PRAYER
THAT OPENS
THE GATE OF
HEAVEN

Evelyn C. Nwosu

WORKBOOK PRESS LLC
187 E Warm Springs Rd,
Suite B285 Las Vegas NV 89119 USA
Website: https://workbookpress.com/
Hotline: 1-888-818-4856
Email: admin@workbookpress.com

Ordering Information:
Quantity sales. Special discounts are available on quantity purchases by corporations, associations, and others. For details, contact the publisher at the address above.

ISBN-13:   978-1-963718-66-9 Paperback Version
                  978-1-965732-05-2 Digital Version

PUB. DATE: 09/03/2024

TABLE OF CONTENTS

ACKNOWLEDGEMENT

I WISH TO FIRST of all express my gratitude to the almighty God, who thought me worthy enough to serve Him, even in this capacity. And for giving me the divine strength with which to complete this work. I also thank the Holy Spirit for the divine enablement, wisdom and strength with which to write this book.

Again I am thanking God for my husband who created an enabling environment for me during the writing of this book.

I thank my wonderful friend Pat Thomas who was always there each time I needed her to help me with IT difficulties.

I give a very big thanks to my brother Sir I. D. Ubani, who facilitated the editing of this book.

I also wish to appreciate a great man of God, Pastor/ Evangelist Jimmy Swaggart of Sonlife ministry, who I believe had influence on the late Archbishop Benson Idahosa, of blessed memory, in whose ministry I gained my spiritual grooming. May I add that if every Christian who is called by the Lord to serve, would answer the Glorious Call like these men of God, I strongly believe that hell would be depopulated, to the glory of God.

And last but not the least, I wish to appreciate my wonderful children, Obichi, and Yeyenta who I fondly call Mina for their encouragement. Also my daughter in-law Ijeoma, who also helped me in answering my IT questions.

I am glad that I finally completed the writing of this book, because the enemy aimed at hindering me, but he is always fighting a lost battle, in that Jesus is always a victor.

INTRODUCTION

T HERE IS NO other route by which human could get connected to God except by prayer. Therefore, praying is the key with which to open the gate of heaven. It is very essential in a believer's Christian race.

Praying to the omnipotent, omnipresent, and omniscient God is what this book is all about. As you read, you will get to understand the meaning of the above titles assigned to God. This book is a prayer manual. You will find it very useful in your spiritual development, and when this happens, your life will change and the gates of heaven will open for you and you will begin to enjoy heavenly blessings. The word Prayer in Hebrew language is *tefillah*, which means *intercession*, and in Greek is *proseuched*, which means vow. Please refer to the chapter on *'Perception of Prayer'* for more explanations.

Prayer is a medium of communication with our creator, the Almighty God, whose name is Jehovah Elohim, the Maker of Heaven and the entire universe without whom the world or man would not be in existence. He is the one who deserves our prayer. He is the Alpha and the Omega (the beginning and the end), All sufficient God. As you proceed, you will discover the importance of prayer and the reason why you should pray. You will also get to know the various types of prayer which will suit your situation, as well as know who God is. Some think that God cannot be reached; this is far from the truth. God can be known as well as reached. I am saying this from experience. God revealed Himself to many of His servants in the Bible, and you will find out this as you read this book. You will also get to know the attributes of God; - if you have not already known.

Prayer is very fundamental in the life of a believer. It will be impossible for one to excel in one's Christian race without a strong adherence to prayer. Many think that they are doing God a favour when they pray; a respectable number of people even think the prayer they say over their meals is enough, that is, for those who even pray at all. They do not know that everything depends on prayer. Some do not pray over their meals; neither do they know why they should pray. All these are because of their ignorance about the importance of prayer. How then do they expect to solve their spiritual problems? Because of ignorance, many fall sick or become demonically oppressed. This is why the Lord says, 'My people perish for lack of knowledge' Hos.4:6. This is my motivation for deciding to write this book. Prayer is the key to solving all your problems, as well as living a victorious Christian life. God gave me a praying ministry, and starting it was not easy, because people were not responding. Even now, the enemy is still fighting to hinder it. I had to go back to God, complaining that people are not responding, and the Lord said, 'It is because they do not know that everything depends on prayer Imagine that!

Another major source of fear is the enemy, the devil. He causes one to develop some indifference towards prayer, by afflicting one with tiredness, nonchalant attitude and the like. I envisage that after you have read this book, your attitude towards prayer shall change for the better. I assure you that you will not remain the same after you have discovered who God is, and you would wish you had known Him earlier.

The Scripture admonishes every Christian to pray without ceasing, and the Lord Jesus Christ, in strong terms, discouraged His disciples from living a life without prayer in order not to fall into temptation. This admonition goes to anyone who calls himself or herself a Christian. Without mincing words, let me say that it is imperative for every Christian to cultivate a consistent and efficacious prayer life, as one without a regular prayer life can hardly be an effective Christian. Praying to our Father in heaven is even more precious than the food we eat. In this turbulent world, we have more than enough to pray for. In our family, for instance, we have our children, husband or wife, finances, health, relations, businesses, neighbours, our spiritual life, friends, and many others, even our enemies to pray for. Once we realise these, we can hardly be barren in our prayer life. Understanding the importance of prayer is of paramount importance; without such understanding, we will never be able to pray effectively, nor be victorious Christian. Therefore the importance of prayer cannot be overemphasised; it is very fundamental in the life of a believer.

CHAPTER ONE

Cultivating A Good Prayer Life

GOOD PRAYER LIFE comes from a good relationship with the Lord Jesus Christ.

In other words, it is having regular fellowship with our Creator. This is why He created us. Remember after He created Adam and Eve and put them in the Garden of Eden, He gave them instruction on how to conduct themselves but when He came down to have fellowship with them, He discovered that they had disobeyed Him. Of course He felt disappointed and became angry with them. This anger had a lot of adverse effect on man's relationship with God.

You will also learn from the experiences of some spirit-filled people of God, who excelled through prayer.

Let me stress again that it is fundamentally necessary for Christians to pray over their meals. Ignorance of this fact makes some people fall sick now and then. This is one of the many strategies of the enemy, apart from hindering them from receiving God's blessings and attaining their destinies. As you read further, you will find out what God says about this.

Knowing how to pray is very important, as some are not knowledgeable in this area. I once heard someone pray thus: 'I pray for my mother, I pray for my sister, I pray for my so and-so.' And that was how she ended her prayer. One does not need to be told that this person did not know how to pray. Of course, this is no prayer. Some people make the mistake of thinking that complaint is the same as prayer. It is therefore no wonder why some find it difficult to pray. As I said earlier, a good prayer life comes from good relationship with the Lord, reading your Bible, attending a church that is Christ centred.

This book is aimed at helping you to overcome your prayer bareness. You will also learn from the experiences of some spirit-filled believers, from people of God who excelled through prayer, including other people's testimonies. It is my prayer that the Spirit of God will touch you as you read this book, and that it will spur you to pray better than you ever did.

I cannot claim that I have always been a prayer warrior, but the habit came through my desire and constant practice and it has given me tremendous victory in my spiritual development. I encourage you therefore to start cultivating this habit of prayer, and the Holy Spirit will help you, because He is sent to help us. He is our helper (our Paraclete).

Procrastination is another weapon which the enemy will use to hinder you from praying. The habit of procrastinating brings about fear and laziness and evokes reasons why you should not pray when you want to. This is the work of the enemy. He will persuade you to postpone your desire to pray and will give you reasons why you should not pray at that time, by telling you, 'Don't worry God knows your problems and He will take care of them.' He will also make you develop indifferent attitude towards prayer, by afflicting you with tiredness, and nonchalant attitude. The Bible tells us that the devil is a liar and that we should therefore resist him. He does this because he knows that once you go to God in prayer, your problems will be solved and God will open your eyes to recognize his evil machinations. I assure you that after you have read this book, your attitude towards prayer shall change for the better, just like mine was changed. Of course, this comes with the help of the Holy Spirit. This is why you need to invite the Lord Jesus Christ into your life, as He is the one to send the Holy Spirit to you. Please refer to the chapter 'A Call to Salvation'.

Knowing how to prepare yourself before you embark on your prayer is very important. Also important are how, where, and when to pray.

You must be aware of different types of prayer and when to apply them, in order to avoid the mistake of praying the right prayer at the wrong time; as a result, we end up not getting the desired result. Our knowledge of them will help make our prayer life easy and interesting.

Our prayer life can change once we acquire this prayer skills. Tiredness can also hinder you from praying effectively. Rest and physical exercise will help put you back in the right spiritual mood appropriate for prayer.

Time also plays an important role in our prayer. There are various times in the day or night when our prayer would be more effective, especially in the mid-day and the mid-night.

Jesus says, 'Men ought always to pray and not to faint.' If Jesus, who is God, but came into this world in human form could take prayer seriously, how much more we, who are mere mortals (dust).

What the Lord said about this book:

Let me reveal to you what the Lord said to me about this book. I was praying one day, when the Lord said to me, 'Please release my book.' I was surprised. and I asked, 'Which book, Lord? And the Lord said, 'I can't wait for you to release my prayer book.' This goes to show how important this book is.

CHAPTER TWO

A Call to Salvation

I T WILL NOT benefit you to read this book if you do not have a good relationship with the Lord Jesus Christ. By this I mean, if He is not your personal Lord and Saviour, and you are not born again, I encourage you to get the best out of this book by making the following confessions below, by inviting Him to rule your life.

But if you are already born again and have accepted the Lord Jesus Christ as your personal Lord and Saviour you can skip this chapter.

Please Make These Confessions:

Lord Jesus, I thank you for loving me, by coming to shed your blood on the cross of Calvary for me, to redeem me from sinful life.

Confess Your Sins Now

The Bible says, 'All have sinned, and come short of the glory of God' (Rom. 3:23 KJV).

Confess: Forgive me of my sins, come into my life, and change me for better.

I want to know you. Reveal yourself to me, that I may know you better.

I promise I am going to worship and serve you and you alone. Help me, Lord. Put your Holy Spirit in me, with the anointing to speak in heavenly languages (tongues), and let the Holy Spirit be my helper.

Come and take over everything about me, my spiritual life, my intellect, my family, my businesses, and everything about me. In Jesus' name, Amen.

'The god Of This World'

May I tell you a short but interesting story The Bible tells us that the world is controlled by a spirit-being, and the Bible calls it, *the god of this world.* The big question is: Who is this god? The answer is in the book of 2 Corinthians. I quote: "But if our gospel be hid, it is hid to them that are lost. In whom the god of this world hath blinded the minds *of them which believe not, lest the light of the glorious gospel of Christ, who is the image of God, should shine unto them*' (2 Cor. 4:3 KJV). Note tlie italicised statement and observe to see the tricks of the devil as stated in the Bible.

The devil or Satan is responsible for your unbelief. He does so by blocking your mind, thereby denying you the glorious light of Jesus Christ. When your mind is unblocked, God will begin to bless you by answering your prayers. This of course takes place when you start worshipping God in spirit and in truth. Remember that the devil will do anything to hind r your spiritual development. Therefore, denounce him by saying these prayers:

Devil, from today, I refuse to have anything to do with you.

Get out of my business, my family, my life (spiritually and physically).

I don't belong to you anymore, in Jesus' name.

Any agreement with you done on my behalf or by me, knowingly or unknowingly, I cancel them in the name of Jesus, who is now my Lord and Saviour. Amen.

Now My Prayer For You:

Father, I thank you for. ....**(enter your name here)** *whom you have beautified with salvation today*.........................**(enter today's date here)**; this should be your spiritual date of birth.

May his or her name be removed from the book of death and be transferred into the book of life, in Jesus' name. thank you, Lord.

Having said this prayer, you are no longer the same person you used to be. You are now a new creation (a son or daughter of God, see John 1:12) because you are now in Christ. The Bible says, 'Therefore, if any man be in Christ, he is a new creature, old things have passed away, behold all things have become new' (2Cor. 5:17). Having now said this prayer, this will be a turning point in your life. You may not believe this now, but write down today's date. Many testimonies await you. This is now your spiritual birthday; it is worth celebrating because you are now qualified to enter into heaven if Jesus Christ comes today. Hallelujh!

Now forgive all those who have offended or sinned against you, so that God can also forgive you. Destroy everything that is of the devil, for instance, charms, images, and things of the sort. If you cannot do it involve your pastor.

CHAPTER THREE

God and His Attributes

Who God Is

TODAY, MANY PEOPLE still wonder who God is, what He looks like, where He lives, and such like. Can you answer any of these questions? If your answer is yes, then you are on your way to heaven. If not, I assure you that by the time you finish reading this book, you will be on your way to heaven. Unfortunately some do not believe in God's existence. In the book of Genesis, it is written: 'In the beginning, God created the heavens and the earth,'...(Gen. 1:1). Arising from the above passage, it is obvious that He is the Creator of heaven and earth and all that is in it, including you and me (man).

God is love. It took a loving God to sacrifice His only Son in order to redeem mankind from Satan: 'For God so loved the world that He gave His only begotten Son, that whoever believes in Him shall not perish but have eternal [everlasting] life. For God did not send His Son into the world to condemn the world, but to save the world through Him, (John 3:16 - 17 NKJV). Yes,

Jesus came into this world in human flesh, in order to die a shameful death for me and you, even the death of the cross, in obedience to His Father's directives. Yes, He gave all even His life in order to save you and me from sin.

God created man in His own image. This means according to the Bible, that we are little gods. But you cannot assume this image if you do not have relationship with the Lord Jesus Christ and do not read and obey what the Bible teaches or walk in the way of the Lord.

The Bible says that we are little gods. If you reject His Son, then you have rejected God because, the two are one and inseparable; you cannot accept one and reject the other. Jesus says, 'I and my Father are one,' (John 10:30).

Some think that God cannot be reached or known; as a result, they make for themselves images to worship. This is so because man inherently craves for some deity to worship. The worship of images is an abomination and a great sin before God. God is omnipotent, omnipresent, and omniscient. He is Omnipresent because He is everywhere at the same time. Omnipotent because He has unlimited or universal power, and Omniscient, because He has all knowledge.

Evidence of God's Existence

Hear what Wayne Grudem said in his book The *Bible Doctrine*: 'All persons everywhere have a deep, inner sense that Godexists, that they are His creatures, and He is their creator. Paul says that even Gentile unbelievers knew God" but did not honour Him as God or give thanks to Him (Romans 1:21). He says that wicked unbelievers have exchanged the truth about God for a lie.'

Creation is further evidence that Godexists: 'In the beginning God created the heaven and the earth' (Gen. 1:1 KJV). If you don't know God, He knows you and is looking for you, because you are the lost sheep; this is Christianity. But people are busy looking for God, this is religion. Since this topic is outside the scope of this book, I shall not go further on this concept.

God's Attributes

God loves man and wants to have fellowship with man; this is why He visited Adam and Eve in the Garden of Eden, only to find out that they had disobeyed Him. The consequence was to hide from God. This explains why some people today do not want to have anything to do with God. God is love: 'For God so loved the world that He gave His only begotten Son that whosoever believes in Him should not perish but have everlasting life.

For God did not send His Son into the world to condemn the world, but that the world through Him might be saved' (John 3:16-17 KJV).

His Promises

God has promised us that whoever comes to Him will never be rejected; neither will the person be forsaken. He says in the book of Jeremiah, 'For I know the thoughts that I think of you, thoughts of peace and not of evil, to give you your future and a hope. Then you will call upon Me and go and pray to Me, and I will listen to you. And you will seek me and find Me when you search for me with all your heart' (Jer. 29:11-13).

God wants to heal our diseases. He wants to provide for us. He wants to protect us. He wants us to prosper, and He wants to give us total well-being. My friends, let me tell you that you cannot have these things outside Jesus Christ in your life.

God's Expectation Of Man

God expects man to believe in Him and obey His commandments. The only way to do this is to study the Word of God, which is the Bible, without which you will not know the will of God for you. As a result, you will be groping in darkness in this world. Jesus says in the Book of John: 'Ye shall know the truth and the truth shall make you free. (John 8:32 KJV). He also says in the book of Jeremiah that when we seek Him with all our heart we shall find Him, (Jere 29: 11-13). This is the only time our prayer will be answered. You see, when we do not worship God in the right way, we will be groping in darkness and our prayers will not be answered. He told us in the scriptures that the prayer of the wicked is an abomination to Him because He also says in His Word (the Bible) that the prayer of the wicked is an abomination to Him. You may say, 'Oh, I am not wicked, because I don't steal, I don't kill,' and so on. But the Bible says that all have sinned and come short of the glory of God.

What God Is Not

People use the things made by God, to create for themselves an image of worship, and call it God. In other words, they are worshiping the creature rather than the Creator. This is idolatry and is an abomination before God. In the Bible, God says, 'I am the First and the Last; besides me there is no other God' (Isa 44:6 NIV). All who make idol are nothing, and the things they treasure are worthless. Those who would speak up for them are blind; they are ignorant, to their own shame' (Is. 44:9-19). He says the same wood you use in making fire for your food is the same thing you use in creating your god, and fall down and worship it. It has mouth but it cannot eat. It has ear but cannot hear and so on. God revealed Himself to Moses by sending him to go and tell Pharaoh on behalf of the children of Israel, to let them go. And Moses asked God, 'Who shall I say has sent me?' God said, 'I AM WHO I AM. Tell him I AM has sent you.' God went further to tell Moses, 'Tell the children of Israel that I am the Lord God of your fathers, the God of Abraham, the God of Isaac, and the God of Jacob.' He added, 'This is my name forever' (Exod. 3:14-15 NIV).

Here the writer is referring to the God of the Bible. This God is not one of the other gods from which we may pick and choose to worship. This God is not to be compared with other deities. He is the Alpha and the Omega (the beginning and the end). He is the creator of heaven and earth, the omnipotent and omniscient God who sent His only begotten Son to come down from heaven (God's abode) in human form and to die a shameful death on the cross, that He may redeem mankind from sin. This God is a triune God; in other words, He is God the Father, God the Son, and God the Holy Spirit. God in three persons it does not mean that they are three gods. Rather it is a Trinity. In other words, God the Father, God the Son and God the Holy Spirit. God incarnated Himself through Jesus. He created the entire universe and all that is in it.

CHAPTER FOUR

Can Man Hear God?

MANY DO NOT believe that God exist, talk less of hearing Him. But I stand here to let you know that man can hear God. The Spirit of God speaks to us when we give our life to Christ. It may not happen immediately. This is why the baptism of the Holy Spirit is very essential or fundamentally important in the life of a born again Christian. How can you serve Him if you don't hear Him? God speaks to us only through His Word in the Bible. This is half the truth, because God still speaks today to His children (committed Christians).

There are many prophets today who hear God and I can personally attest to this, but one does not need to be a prophet to hear God. God says in His book, the Bible, 'My sheep hear my voice (John 10:27 KJV). As you can see this is in the New Testament.

Hearing from God

Jesus told us that the Holy Spirit, which is the Spirit of God, will not tell us something of His own, but that which comes from God. Hear what Jesus said about the Holy Spirit: "*Nevertheless J tell you the truth. It is to your advantage that I go away; for if I do not go away, the Helper will not come to you; but if I depart, I will send Him to you. However, when He the Spirit of truth, has come, He will guide you into all truth; for He will not speak on His own authority, but whatever he hears He will speak; and He will tell you things to come,*" (John 16:7&13.....). Therefore, if the Holy Spirit tells you what He heard from God, it follows that we have heard from God.

At the first time I heard from God, I had not given my life to Christ, I was just a committed Christian; a regular church goer who prayed often. I followed in the footsteps of my mother and besides my father was a pastor. They had a very big influence upon my life. God used to speak to me even then, and the first time I heard from Him was when He asked me the type of man I would want to marry. The question came to me unexpectedly. It was an audible voice; I did not see the person talking to me. But I knew the question was for me, because I was all alone at the time. I knew it was God speaking to me. I then began to ponder in my mind the qualities of the man I would like to marry. This was in my early teens. But before God spoke to me there was a man whose picture used to appear in the newspapers, and I used to admire it. This was when I was much younger, I used to fancy marrying a man like him. Little did I know that Godknew what was in my mind.

He started searching for a man that looked like

the man for me. In fact I had forgotten about the voice I heard until I saw my husband. God knows your heart's desire, and He is ever willing to give it to you. I had not mentioned this testimony to my husband until today, and when I enquired from my husband if he knew the man, his reply was in the affirmative. It was then that I told my husband about the voice from God, and he smiled. We have been married for forty-eight years.

My husband is almost everything I asked God for in a man. This means that once your heart is knitted to God's, God can speak to you; only be attentive. But be careful; the devil also speaks. How to differentiate is that he will tell you to do evil; therefore, always compare what you hear with the Word of God.

Many do not believe that God exists, talk less of hearing Him. But I stand here to tell you that man can hear God. It is the Spirit of God that speaks to us, and this happens when one gives one's life to Christ. It may not happen immediately. This is why the baptism of the Holy Spirit is very important in the life of a Believer.

CHAPTER FIVE

How Jesus Introduced the Holy Spirit

GOD REVEALED HIMSELF in His Son, Jesus Christ, who promised His disciples before He was crucified on the Cross of Calvary that He would send the Holy Spirit to them, (Acts 1:45). This was what happened on the Day of Pentecost (Acts 2:112). This promise is also made to all who believe in Him.

In the book of John, Jesus Christ said:

> "Nevertheless I tell you the truth; It is expedient for you that I go away: for if I go riot away, the comforter will not come unto you: but if I depart, I will send Him unto you. And when He is come, He will reprove the world of sin, and of_righteousness and of judgement" (John 16:7-8 KJV)

Clearly, Jesus was promising to send the Holy Spirit to His disciples. This Holy Spirit according to Jesus is the Comforter and Helper or Paraclete. Once you believe in Christ, you become His disciple and automatically are entitled to receive the Holy Spirit.

The deity of Jesus Christ:

Theologically speaking, Jesus is the only Son of God, begotten through the Virgin Mary. He is the Saviour sent by God into this sinful world in human flesh, to die a shameful death on the Cross of Calvary, that those who would believe in his name and also exercise their faith in His atonement death might be redeemed from sinful nature.

He is the head of the Church and the key to the foundation of the Church. Christ is preeminent, first and foremost in everything, and the Christian's life should reflect that priority. Believers are rooted in Him, alive in Him, hidden in Him, and complete in Him; it is utterly inconsistent for them to live their life without Him. Clothed in His love, with His peace ruling in their hearts, they are equipped to make Christ first in every area of life (Austin Phelps, The Still Hour)

Jesus is the only Son of God, who came on this earth in human flesh. The book of Isaiah, refers to Jesus as "Wonderful Counsellor, Mighty God, Everlasting Father, Prince of Peace" (Isa 9:6). He is our Lord and Saviour, our Redeemer and the Messiah. He is the Way, the Truth, and the Life (John 14:6).

He created everything that exists on earth. He is: 'the Word and the Light.' I quote from the Word of God:

> In the beginning was the Word and the Word was with God and the Word was God. The same was in the beginning with God. All things were made by Him, and without Him was not anything made that was made. In Him was life and the life was the light of men. And the Light shineth in darkness, and darkness comprehended it not. There was a man sent from God, whose name was John. The same came for a witness, to bear witness of the light, that all men through Him might believe. He was not that light, but was sent to bear witness of that Light. That was the true Light, which lighteth every man that cometh into the world. He was in the world, and the world was made by Him, and the world knew Him not. But as many as received Him, to them gave He power to become the sons of God, even to them that believe in His name. Which were born, not of blood, nor of the will of man, but of God, (John 1: 1-13, KJV)

From this passage, you will observe that Jesus and God (His Father) are the same and one person. Therefore Jesus was Godincarnate. Secondly, it is only by accepting Jesus Christ as your personal Lord and

Saviour can you become a child of God. You should, sincerely invite Him into your life, and regularly attend a Bible focused Church. By this I mean where Salvation through Jesus Christ is preached.

CHAPTER SIX

Perception of Prayer

I WOULD LIKE to define *prayer as 'the one who prays.)* *Prayer* is also the act of praying, entreaty, a petition to or communicating with a deity. In this book, our reverence is unto the Almighty God, He is the one to be prayed to. Prayer is also an act of worship, a solemn request for help, an expression of thanks, or a petition addressed to our God.

Terminology Of Prayer

The terminology of prayer in the Bible is very rich and varied. The Hebrew word for prayer is *tefillah,* which means *intercession or supplication.* This term, refers to prayer in general terms, while in Greek it means *proseuche* or vow. This also could be misleading, as vow could mean 'pledge or promise.

However, for the purpose of this book, prayer means to pray or to communicate with Jehovah the Almighty God. It is important that we know the etymology or the original meaning of the word *prayer* for better understanding and effectiveness. The Old Testament definition of prayer is derived from the

Hebrew version while the New Testament is from the Greek version of the Bible, it is therefore always vital to find out the context and the root of any statement or word in the Bible. Again, for the purpose of this book, and in the perspective of a Christian, prayer is defined as a solemn request to God Almighty for help. It could take the form of worship, praise, thanksgiving, petition, supplication, and so on.

Everything Depends On Prayer

As I said earlier when God initially called me to the Prayer Ministry, it was not easy for me and I wished He had given me another ministry. Consequently, I went to God in prayer to inform Him that people were not responding, and God said to me: 'It is because they do not know that *everything depends on prayer*.' This confirms why Jesus always prayed. On the day of His crucifixion He prayed so much that the sweat which flowed from His body became as thick as blood. This further goes to emphasize the importance of prayer.

Prayer Should Be A Dialogue

Prayer is a two-way communication process. And not a one way process. We worship, or send our petition, to God; therefore, if we are spiritual enough, we should be able to receive answers from Him in return. But this may not always be the case nor do answers come immediately. In other words, some answers to our prayer may take longer. God does things at His own time because He knows best. Therefore we must be patient and steadfast.

In the book of Isaiah, God says, 'For *My thoughts are not your thoughts, neither are your ways my ways*.' (Is.55: 8-9).God will always be God, and man cannot force God to do anything. Ours is to pray, humble ourselves, and wait. As earlier stated, if we are spiritual enough, we should be able to know when the answer to our prayer is delivered. I speak from experience.

Why Some Find It Difficult To Pray

Some Christians find prayer burdensome, because they do not know the importance of prayer. Again, their approach is usually one-way exercise. As a result, they do not know how to receive from God. In other words, they do not listen to the Holy Spirit of God while praying. The Bible told us that God is a spirit: *God is a spirit and they that worship Him must worship him in spirit and in truth*," (John 4:24 KJV). God has even invited us to come and reason with him, and we can reason with the Lord by going down on our knees. As we pray we should realise that we are dealing with a spiritual being (our creator), and therefore, we should be alert in our spirit, conscious of the fact that He is beside us. If you are conscious of the fact that the Lord is by your side, you will certainly be more relaxed and free in your communication with Him. The emphasis should be on talking with God and not talking to God.

You should know that God cares about you and your problems and is listening to you with a desire to help you, no matter what the problems may be. Therefore you must listen to His responses, they may not be audible. This is why you should be alert in the spirit. Sometimes God talks to us through our spirit.

Again, the word prayer is a powerful word, which makes the devil quiver. Because you are communicating with your heavenly Father. This makes the devil jealous. This is why he will always hinder you from praying, by making you feel or say things like 'God knows my needs, so I do not need to pray, He does this because he knows that when you pray, God will answer your prayer and will consequently bless you. Furthermore, he will not be able to afflict you because God will show you a way out of your problems. Most especially, he will not let you pray because when you do, his kingdom suffers a quake and a setback, dislocation, and there will be confusion and frustration, in his camp. Hallelujah.

He does this because he knows that when you pray, God will answer your prayer and will consequently bless you. Furthermore, he will not be able to afflict you because God will show you a way out of your problems. Most especially, he will not let you pray because when you do, his kingdom suffers a quake and a setback, dislocation, and there will be confusion and frustration, in his camp. Hallelujah.

Heiler's View On Prayer:

On the subject of prayer, permit me to quote from Heiler's book on prayer and the second from Karl Rahner's, volume 3 of his *Theological Investigations Heiler writes 'In exposition of prayer in personal religion, it is almost exclusively Biblical and Christian personalities have to be taken into account. Christianity including the prophetic religion of the Old Testament is the peculiar home of personal prayer,'* Soderblom remarks, or it is, as Bousset says, 'Simply the religion of prayer, that is the religion in which prayer is the focus of personal piety. To be a Christian, he continued, means to be one who prays. Heiler went further to quote Luther as follows: 'As a shoemaker makes a shoe and a tailor makes a coat, so ought a Christian to pray. Prayer is the daily business of a Christian." Furthermore, he quoted Luther again: 'To pray is a strange work which no one but the Christian perform and yet it has been very common in the world.'

The author went further to remind us that the above quotation reminds us of what the historian looking to the past can't tell us about the place of prayer in Christianity. By contrast, it is interesting to note the rather different judgement of a modern theologian that went further to quote Karl Rahner in his essay 'The Apostolate of prayer' as follows: *'Do we Christians really believe in the power of prayer? Believe, that is, in its power on the earth and not merely in some distant heavenly place of God? Is our thinking still sufficiently anthropomophic to make us dare to believe that we can by our bawling weeping move the heart of God to intervene in this world? Or has our thinking become so abstract, so spiritless that we will allow to prayer no other value than that of a tranquilizer, or recognise it as no more than affirmation of our hope for a success beyond this life?'*

However, our prayer of petition is seriously a problem. Its practice is now almost exclusively confined to ordinary people. It is found only where a 'primitive religiosity' holds sway, which in the opinion of the more sophisticated has not quite grasped the fact that we cannot ask anything of God, since He is in the ultimate analysis an inexorable Fate. These others, the clever ones who do not form part of this folk become 'primitive' only when they have their backs to the wall. Then they will pray. (An excerpt from Church Service Society.org, November 1976).

What Prayer Is Not

Prayer is not enchantment, nor is it incantation, or swearing, as some people may imagine. The prayer we say over our meals is important but is not enough; it is only to thank God for the food and ask Him to bless it. We have many needs in our lives which we should pray for. God our Father is always ready and willing to hear our problems. Therefore, do not allow the enemy, the devil, to hinder you; you must always resist him.

Why You Must Pray Over Your Meals:

It is important for us to pray over our meals or food for various reasons; one of which is that the food we eat pass through many hands and channels. Again some people dedicate their businesses, for instance shops, farms, and factories to the deities they worship. But God says that He is the one who created the herbs, the animals and other raw materials with which the food we eat are produced, therefore we should not be afraid, but just pray over them and eat. This is very true, as I have heard a story where someone bought some processed food from a market, as the person was carrying the food home from the market, the person heard the food saying to each other: 'Do not squash me.' This may seem untrue and spooky, but this news went round for a long time, and people believed it.

CHAPTER SEVEN

Know Who You Are Directing Your Prayer To

P RAYER IS ALWAYS directed to God. Some people do not know who they are praying to. One should not pray to a deity one does not know. Our prayer should always be to God, our Creator.

Some Worship What They Know Not

The Lord Jesus told the woman at the well: *Ye worship what you do not know*," (John 4:22a NKJV). Some people pray to what they do not know. In the Bible, Saint Paul addressed a similar problem when he saw the people of Athens praying to an unknown god. Of course, he seized the opportunity to minister the gospel of the Lord Jesus Christ to them. So also today, many people pray to what they do not know, out of ignorance. God said in the book of Hosea, 'My people perish for lack of knowledge' (Hos. 4:6). God Almighty is the only one we should pray to and worship, *Our Father which is in heaven*) as the Lord Jesus taught us. His other names are Jehovah Elohim, self-existent God, the I AM THAT I AM, Jehovah El-Shaddai, the all-sufficient God, and the Creator of heaven and earth. He it was that sent His only begotten Son, the Lord Jesus Christ, into this sinful world to die a shameful death on behalf of mankind, even the death of the cross, that man might be saved and consequently inherit eternal life through faith in His atonement death on the cross. This was the way in which He showed His love to us: '*For God so loved the world that He gave His only begotten Son; that whosoever believes in Him should not perish but have everlasting lifen* (John 3:16 NKJV). This is the triune God, that is, the Godin three persons: God the Father, God the Son and God the Holy Spirit. He is the God who revealed Himself to Moses at Mount Horeb. He is the only one we should pray to and the only one whose name we should reverence, honour, worship, praise, and be grateful to, every minute of our lives.

How To Identify Your Adversary

The Bible warns us not to forget that the devil is our adversary, and he roams to and fro, seeking whom to devour. The devil knows that when you pray, the Lord will answer your prayer and consequently bless you. Therefore, he will do anything to stop you from praying. Why does he do this? He does it because he is jealous of your relationship with the Lord. With this in mind, we must earnestly resist him every minute of our lives, because his goal is to pull us down. The only weapon we have to resist him is constantly rertewing our relationship with the Lord, through prayer.

To be in right standing with the Lord demands steadfastness, a fortified prayer life, study of the Word, obedience, and living a holy and righteous life. Our victory is in our confessing and acting out the Word of God, not forgetting our testimonies and the sprinkling of the blood of Jesus. Also through membership of a Bible believing Church which teaches the Lord's salvation as well as living the life of a true Christian, because there are many who call Jesus with their lips but do not live their lives according to His doctrines.

How To Resist The Devil

The devil targets your heart through your mind. He does this by letting in evil thoughts into your mind. If you do not reject such thought immediately, it finds its way into your heart. When this happens, lust could turn into adultery, anger could turn into hatred and further into resentment, and so on. Therefore, Keep your heart from being defiled. In order to be an effective Christian, you need to constantly resist the enemy so he doesn't defile you through sin. Hear what the Bible says:

Are you also without understanding? Do ye not perceive that whatever thing from without entereth into the man, it cannot defile him; because it entereth not into his heart, but into the belly, and goeth out into the draught, purging all meats? And He said, that which cometh out of the man, that defileth the man. For from within, out of the heart of men, proceed evil thoughts, adulteries, fornications, murders, stealing, covetousness, wickedness, deceit, lasciviousness, an evil eye, blasphemy, pride, foolishness. All these evil things come from within, and defile the man. (Mark 7:7-20, KJV)

This sh@ws that what defiles us is not necessarily what we eat. The above listed sins will hinder our prayers from being answered, because the Lord says that the prayer of the wicked is an abomination unto Him. God regards a sinner as a wicked person. Sin defiles man.

CHAPTER EIGHT

When, What, Where, and How to Pray

When To Pray:

F OR EFFECTIVENESS, IT is always necessary to know when to pray, except if you are spiritually led otherwise.

Learning from Jesus' Example

Jesus had a consistent prayer life. On the day He was crucified, He left His disciples and went to pray in the garden of Gethsemane. It is only through prayer that you can tell your problems to God, and in return expect answers.

Many Christians are not sure when they should pray. They tell you that the Bible says one should go into one's closet (house) to pray behind the closed doors. This may be true, but one also need to know the context under which the statement was made. Jesus made the statement because the Pharisees liked to show off by praying in the public places, like markets, and the road sides, so that people would see them.

But I believe that we should pray when we feel led by the Holy Spirit or feel the need to pray. We are admonished in the book of Thessalonians to pray without ceasing (lThess. 5:17 KJV). This means that we can pray each time we are led to pray. Some may ask: How do you know? You will know if you are always sensitive in the spirit, because delay may be dangerous. See what the Bible says about living in the spirit:

> For those who live according to the flesh set their minds on the things of the flesh, but those who live according to the Spirit, the things of the Spirit . . . So then those who are in the flesh cannot please God ... But if the Spirit of Him who raised Jesus from the dead dwells in you, He who raised Christ from the dead will also give life to your mortal bodies through His Spirit who dwells in you, (Rom. 8:5, 8:11 NKJV).

The emphasis here is mine. The book of Romans chapter 8 is one of the passages in the Bible which inspires me. I like to read it very often, because it helps me to develop my spiritual life. I encourage you to make this passage one of your favourites too. This way you certainly would be able to fellowship with the Holy Spirit, and it will enable you to excel in your spiritual life. I tell you that if you know when to pray, you will have the devil under your feet.

When, What, Where, and How to Pray

I would like to pause here to give you a testimony of my experience while travelling with a friend who invited me to attend her mother in-law's burial. I will not disclose her identity, but this took place in Nigeria. On the day of the burial, we set out together with her husband driving the car. As we approached a certain spot near a bridge, I had a strong urge to plead the blood of Jesus over the car, but I hesitated as I did not want to appear too spiritual. incidentally my friend and her husband were also very strong spiritually. As we approached the bridge on a high speed the urge became stronger, even to the extent of almost forcing itself out of my mouth, it was then that I was compelled to gently say out the words: 'I cover this car with the blood of Jesus.' To my surprise, the car immediately began to swerve from left to right with my friend's husband almost loosing control of the car. At this point we were right on top of the bridge. It happens that the river is fast flowing; besides, accidents often took place in that spot: We were saved because I obeyed the Holy Spirit of God by speaking out the words into the spiritual, and the Lord used it to perform His miracle.

Brethren, it pays to be in the spirit, and it is therefore important to pray when you are led to.

The scripture says that a man that is born of the Spirit is like a wind; you do not know where he or she is going or where he or she is coming from.

That which is born of the flesh is flesh, and that which born of Spirit is spirit. Do not marvel that I said to you, You must be born again.' The wind blows where it wishes, and you hear the sound of it, but cannot tell where it comes from and where it goes. So is everyone who is born of the Spirit, (John 3:6-8 NKJV).

This statement is telling us that a spirit -filled Christian is at most times doing things that may seem strange to a carnal person. This is true, as long as it is not being faked.

Prayer Is Discipline

Prayer is a discipline, says Cindy Jacobs, in her book *Possessing the Gates of Your Enemies*. It takes discipline to develop a life of prayer. It is important to note that prayer that reaches God begins and ends with worship. Again, praise induces worship; if you want to pray and are unable, go into praise, and definitely, you will find yourself in the mood to pray. This habit, if maintained, will certainly make your prayer less tiresome. Pastor Adeboye of the Redeemed Christian Church of God, in his book *Spiritual Warfare*, had this to say: Separate yourself; no man that warreth entangleth himself [or herself] with the affairs of this world' (2Tim. 2:3). This is very important, because you do not want people to drag you behind spiritually. Jesus was always separating Himself, even from His disciples. You do not want people to drag you down spiritually.

Sever yourself from any relationship which will drag you down spiritually.

Have A Regular Prayer Time

Make enough time for your prayer; do not be in a hurry. God warned me some time ago that I should not hurry out of His presence. In effect God is telling us that He enjoys our fellowship with Him. It is better to have an altar or a place set aside in your house, set aside for communion with your Creator. It could be your bedroom, if you are alone in the house, or any other convenient spot, but be consistent. Again, endeavour to have a regular time if it is possible. This enables the Angels to be ready at your command. It also facilitates response to your prayer from the Lord. This is not to say that all your prayers will receive immediate attention; some prayers may take longer to yield fruits. But remember that the Lord says that before we pray we should believe that He has already answered us even though sometimes it may take time to be answered while some may be ignored, if such prayers are for selfish reasons. Imagine if God answered certain of our prayers, we would perhaps regret praying.

Where You Should Pray

Again, the Bible admonishes us to pray without ceasing; it follows therefore, that wherever we may be, we should pray if the Holy Spirit leads or directs us to do so. Recall the testimony I made regarding the journey to the burial of my friend's mother-in-law.

May I share this short but related testimony? One day, the Holy Spirit directed me to pray for one of my aunts, whose name the Holy Spirit mentioned. This my aunt lived in a city different from where I lived. I had not heard from her or seen her for a long time, so I was not sure what to pray about, nor did I know of any problem she might be having. All sorts of thought flashed through my mind. Could she be in trouble or could she be sick? Not being sure, I asked the Holy Spirit to lead me, and I prayed first in the spirit (tongues). Then I was led to pray for her to be delivered out of any problems she might have been encountering including ill health. After this prayer, it took a long while, about three or four weeks, before I saw her. She had no access to telephones at the time, because mobile phones were not available at that time.

In course of our conversation, she told me that she had not been well, and that she had almost died; and this period of her ill health coincided with the period when the Holy Spirit led me to pray for her. I then informed her that the Holy Spirit had revealed it to me. If I had delayed praying for her at the time the Holy Spirit asked me to pray, I would probably have lost her then, even though she had recently gone to be with the Lord. This underscores the importance of being spiritual and acting without delay when we are led to do something.

When Not To Pray

It may be wise to examine our mood before we decide to embark on a serious prayer. Do not attempt to pray when fear grips you or when you are anxious or when you are excited about something, because it will be difficult to pray effectively.

It is important to note that fear is the weapon of the enemy, the devil. He uses it to confuse the children of God; and can use it to weaken us spiritually. In such situations, I advise that you invite someone who has the spirit of God to support you in prayer. It could be a friend, a brother or brothers in the Church, your pastor, or an elder in the Church.

The following conditions could trigger fear in you and cause you to be overly excited: bereavement of a loved one, difficult labour of a loved one, sudden accident involving a friend or a relation, serious and unexpected ill health likely to lead to death, and such like. These conditions could cause nervousness; leading to, your loss of concentration. It is therefore difficult to pray effectively under such situations. I am saying this from personal experience. Have you ever pondered why doctors are not allowed to carry out surgical operations on their loved ones. This is one of the reasons.

Praying for Others

Our prayer can help change situations in our nuclear family, community, and even our nation. In my community in Nigeria, a non denominational fellowship is held regularly, say monthly where people gather together under one umbrella once a month to pray, irrespective of one's denomination, and the Lord is using it to do great things in that Community. Souls are being saved, churches are being impacted positively, ministers who did not understand the meaning of being born again are learning and applying it in their churches, thereby affecting the lives of their congregations positively. As you pray, God will do the same in your Community. The Bible admonishes us to pray for those in authority; be they at national or local levels, and the leaders of all establishments in our country.

Silent Prayer

You may never know the extent the Lord wants to help you, until you get close to Him. Prayer does not necessarily depend on shouting, jumping, or doing any manner of acrobatics. Silent prayer is as effective as verbal prayer; and please don't use the opportunity to pray bad prayer.

God has used silent prayer to bless me. Sometimes, I think that it is more readily effective than verbal prayer. It is like speaking in the heavenly language (tongues), because the enemy does not know what you are praying about and therefore he cannot hinder you.

CHAPTER NINE

Developing a Good Relationship with God

P RAYER IS A relationship with God. A renowned man of God by the name of Adrian Rogers, who has now gone to be with the Lord, had this to say about prayer: Prayer is not a monologue [that is, an address, a speech, or a sermon], but a dialogue, a two-way business with God. In other words, as you talk to God, you should expect God to talk back to you. However, this may not always be the case, but a good Christian should always form the habit of spending time with the Lord in prayer. This habit will not come easy, but requires perseverance and constant practice.

Prayer should be a refreshing time with our Father in heaven; He desires to have fellowship with us. This was why He put Adam and Eve in the Garden of Eden, but they wasted the opportunity and brought a curse upon man. In the book of John, we read how God loves us so much that He sent His only begotten Son, Jesus Christ, to come to this earth to die in our place:

For God so loved the world that He gave His only begotten Son, that whosoever believes in Him should not perish but have everlasting life (John 3:16 KJV). What a way to exhibit love.

How to Recognize the Presence of God

It pays to be able to distinguish the voice of God from that of Satan during our prayers. The Bible says that the devil pretends to be an angel of light: 'And no wonder! For Satan himself transforms himself into an angel of light' (2Cor. 11:13 KJV). This means that he will pretend to be the Holy Spirit by speaking to you during your prayer. You should always enquire to be sure it is the voice of God that you are hearing, by asking, 'God, is that you talking to me?' If it is the Spirit of God talking to you, He will confirm it and embolden you the more to pray. But if it is the enemy pretending to be the Lord, that voice will just cease instantly because, the devil is timid. Therefore, once he knows that you have recognized his tricks, he will run away. But that will not be the end of him. He behaves like a fly; he does not go for good; he hovers around to find another opportunity for a come-back. This why you always need to e vigilant. Bind every spirit that is not the spirit of God and cast it out of your prayer arena before you start your prayer.

This calls for regular study and meditation on the Word of God; otherwise, you will fall prey to the enemy, the devil. At one time, I was praying, and the Lord opened my eyes to see some insects which looked like mosquitoes in appearance, flying around where I was praying, with their bellies filled with human blood and protruding. As I beheld them, the Holy Spirit said to me, //'These are not ordinary mosquitoes, they are v demons.' Could you have imagined that?

How To Attract The Presence Of God

Recognising the presence of God during your prayer brings supreme delight. Obedience to the Word of God attracts the presence of God. This is the first secret of prayer. Those who were committed in prayer recognised God's presence: people like Paul and Silas in the prison, Daniel (whose answer to prayer was hindered prayed until an angel brought the answer to him). Abraham (entertained angels), Jacob (wrestled with an angel until the angel blessed him), and Moses (whose face shone so much that the children of Israel could not behold it because of the glory of God). These things happened because they were always in the presence of God .

Feel Free In His Presence

One's earthly father would not harm any of his children because he loves them, but God gave His beloved Son to die for us. Imagine how you feel when you are in the presence of your earthly father because you know that he loves you; you feel so free and want to tell him everything on your mind. This is how we should feel in the presence of our heavenly Father when we pray. His eyes follow us wherever we go. Please read

Psalm 91, Jeremiah 29:11. In the book of Isaiah, God invites us to come and reason with Him: *Come now) and let us reason together; says the Lord. Though your sins are like scarlet) they shall be as white as snow: though they are red as crimson) they shall be like wool* (Is. 1:18 AMP).

Also in the book of Isaiah He said: '*If you are willing and obedient) you will eat the fruit of the land/* (Is. 1:19 AMP). Yes, we are always willing, but are we also obedient?

I wish to point out that when God gave me the ministry of prayer, I was really struggling with it, and had to go back to God, to complain that people were not responding, Guess what God said, He said, 'It is because they do not know that everything depends on prayer.' I wish therefore to remind you here that *everything depends on prayer.*

CHAPTER TEN

Solving Your Problems Through Prayer

W E PRAY FOR various reasons. In addition to having fellowship with our creator, we seek solution to our problems through prayer. Such problems include:

Health

There is a common adage which says that health is wealth. And that cannot be denied, because a sick person cannot acquire wealth. One has good health when he or she is said to be hale, sound or whole, in body soul and mind, and is free from physical pain and enjoy (total well-being).

Good health is one of the gifts the Lord has freely given to His children. God said in His Word, that healing is His children's bread. In the Book of Isaiah, we are told: By the stripes of the Lord Jesus, we are healed: 'He was wounded for our transgressions, He was bruised for our iniquities. The chastisement for our peace was upon Him. And by His stripes we are healed'

(Isa. 53:5 NKJV). Apostle Peter in his epistle also emphasized, 'By His stripes you were healed.' This is a good and relevant portion to claim. When the enemy threatens you with illness, all you need to do is to remind him of this passage and he will become powerless and will flee. This is what Jesus suffered for, that we maybe whole in our bodies and have total well-being, which include your finances and businesses and many more.

It is said that Jesus was given thirty-eight stripes before His crucifixion, and that each stripe represented a kind of ailment. In the book of 3 John, the Lord said, 'Beloved, I pray that you may prosper in all things and be in health, just as your soul prospers' (3John 1:2, NKJV). I like the old King James version of which says: 'Beloved, I wish above all things that you may prosper, and be in health, even as your soul prospers.'

Peace of Mind

The benefit of being a child of God are enormous. Jesus is the Prince of Peace; therefore, every child of God is entitled to have peace from above, that peace that passes all understanding. Whenever the enemy, the devil attempts to cause you pain or stress, all you need to do is to remind him what the Lord Jesus suffered on the cross, for your peace; you should lay claim on it through prayer and your confession based on the Word of God. Tell him that when the Lord Jesus said on the cross, 'It is finished,' it included your peace of mind and whatever the enemy is afflicting you with.

Do you know that your prayer can turn your enemies into your friends, and consequently enable you enjoy a peaceful life? The Bible says, 'If it be possible, be at peace with all men.' The fewer enemies you have, the more peace of mind you will have. Therefore, endeavour to have as few enemies as possible. It is possible only by being forgiving and tolerant.

Your Household

As a child of God, you have authority over your household; apply it and decree it and so shall it be. The Bible says in the book of Job: "Ye shall decree a thing and it shall be established. The angels of the Lord will honour your command. I am not recommending they should be worshipped but tell them what you want them to do for you; remember every believer is entitled to a ministering angel. This is their work, provided we recognise and involve them. God will never get involved in your problems if you do not invite Him. Let me tell you a short testimony in this regard. I was once experiencing difficulty in my life, and I was busy meditating on the problem instead of praying. Eventually, I decided to pray, and I could not believe what I heard while praying. The Lord said to me: 'Alright, now that you have decided to come to me! In other words, He was watching me to see what I would do' Do you know that after that prayer, the problem just disappeared?

Marriage

Marriage is one institution where the devil performs havoc. This is so because he knows that a family that prays together can achieve wonderful things. The Bible says that one can chase a thousand, and two can chase ten thousand. This is why the devil is afraid of families; hence, he tries very much to destabilise marriages. Spouses should endeavour to be constantly in agreement to enable them pray together, because two cannot pray together except they agree. Much can be achieved when couples pray together. Time will not permit me here to testify to what we were able to achieve in my family through praying with my husband.

All spouses should therefore pray for one another, because our strength lies in praying together. One spouse may be more prayerful than the other.

Some spouses are too lazy to pray, to the point that they do not even pray before they go to bed. In such cases, more prayerful spouse should pray and cover the other spouse in his or her prayer before bedtime. The Bible says that while men sleep, the enemy comes to sow tar. When this happens, do not be surprised if such a spouse wakes up in the morning and starts behaving in funny way through his or her actions or utterances. Such actions or utterances could spark quarrels, which otherwise could have been prevented through prayer.

Pray for your children, relations (yours and your spouse's), friends, neighbours, colleagues, even your enemies (your prayers can change them)

CHAPTER ELEVEN

Corporate Prayer

W E READ IN the book of Acts how the disciples of Jesus had a Pentecostal experience in Jerusalem where they were together after Jesus had resurrected. The Holy Spirit came upon all of them in the form of a cloven tongue of fire and baptised them with the evidence of speaking in tongues.

> *And when the day of Pentecost was fully come, they were all with one accord in one place. And suddenly there came a sound from heaven, as of a rushing mighty wind, and it filled all the house where they were sitting, And there appeared unto them like as of fire, and it sat upon each of them. And they were all filled with the Holy Ghost, and began to speak with other tongues as the Spirit gave them utterance. (Acts 2:1-4 KJV)*

Notice that there were other nationalities in the room where this incident took place. For instance, residents of Mesopotamia, Judea, Cappadocia, Pontus and Asia, Phrygia, Pamphylia, Egypt and parts of

Libya near Cyrene, Rome (both Jews and converts of Judaism), Crete, and Arabia. These people were amazed and perplexed, and they asked, What does this mean?" They heard the apostles speaking in their various languages; for instance, there were Parthians, Medes, Elamites, Asians, Judeans, and others, and these people heard the apostles speaking in their native languages and they began to be amazed and marvelled, saying to one another, Look, are not all these who speak Galileans? Some even accused them of being drunk. Then Peter told them that the menwere not drunk and that this was what prophet Joel meant:

> But Peter standing up with the eleven lifted up his voice and said unto them, ye men of Judea, and all ye that dwell in Jerusalem, be this known unto you, and hearken to my words: For these are not drunken as ye suppose, seeing it is but the third hour of the day. But this is that which was spoken by the prophet Joel: And it shall come to pass in the last days, saith God, 'I will pour out of my Spirit upon all flesh; and your sons and your daughters shall prophesy and your young men shall see visions, and your old men shall dream dreams: And on my servants and on my handmaidens I will pour out in those days of my Spirit: and they shall prophesy: And I will shew wonders in heaven above, and sign in the earth beneath:

blood and fire, and vapour of smoke: The sun shall be turned into darkness, and the moon into blood before that great and notable day of the Lord come, and it shall come to pass that whosoever shall call on the name of the Lord shall be saved.' (Acts 2:5-21, KJV)

The above experience was made possible because the apostles were together; this goes to confirm why we should always be in the midst of brethren who are equally filled with the Spirit of God. This radiates corporate anointing and is spiritually very effective. This is why the Lord says that we should not forsake the assembling of the brethren; it is very powerful. This without gainsaying can bring down the presence and the power of God tremendously.

As can be seen above, corporate anointing can be very effective. The power of God came down powerfully because the disciples gathered themselves together for prayer in one accord; in other words, they were all in agreement.

Remember that tongues come only when people are praying. I believe they were praying, because the disciples of Jesus Christ were always praying. Remember Paul and Silas in the prison; also, Peter was miraculously released from the prison by the angel of God because he was praying. Every believer should have a prayer partner for easy breakthrough. The Bible says one can chase a thousand and two can chase ten thousand.

Pardon me here; sometimes I find it difficult to interchange Christians for believers, the reason being that there are some religious sects who claim to be Christians but do not live their lives according to the doctrines of Christ; therefore, I choose to use the word *believers* to specially distinguish those Christians who live their lives based on the doctrines of Christ.

Power In Your Faith

You must have faith in the name and the doctrine of Jesus Christ, before you can pray to God and expect an answer: '*But without faith it is impossible to please Him) for he who comes to Him must believe that He is) and that He is a rewarder of those who diligently seek Him*' (Heb. 11:6 KJy). Secondly, you must be in the right standing with the Lord before you can expect your prayer to ascend unto God. The Bible says that the prayer of the wicked (ungodly, sinner) is an abomination unto God. In Proverbs, it is written: '*The sacrifice of the wicked is an abomination to the Lord) But the prayer of the righteous is His delight*' (Prov. 15:8 KJV). In other words, you cannot pray to God without having faith in Him and expect an answer. God answers the prayer of a righteous (born-again) person. The Bible says: The effectual fervent prayer of the righteous avails much (James 5:16b KJV). The Amplified Version puts it this way: 'The earnest [heartfelt, continued] prayer of a righteous man makes tremendous power available [dynamic in its working].'

CHAPTER TWELVE

Power in the Word

T HERE IS POWER in the Word of God, He honours His Word above His name. Therefore, the importance of the Word of God in your prayers cannot be overemphasised.

God has empowered His Word and whenever we apply His Word into our prayer, we are guaranteed a breakthrough. The scripture tells us that the Word of God is quick and powerful, sharper than any two-edged sword: *For the Word of God is quick and powerful) and sharper than any two-edged sword. Piercing even to the dividing asunder of soul and spirit and of joints and marrow and is a discerner of thoughts and intents of the heart'* (Heb. 4:12 KJV). Therefore, if you want a quick response from God, always remind Him of His Word and His promises.

The Healing Of A Woman With The Spirit Of Lunacy

The testimony of a woman who was healed of the spirit of lunacy is a very good example. Sometime ago I was in my office, in Port Harcourt, Rivers State of Nigeria, when a work colleague who happened to be a member of the workplace Fellowship - 'The Redeemed Civil Servants Fellowship' which I founded, approached me to discuss her problem. Looking worried she narrated that her daughter was seriously ill and was behaving like a mad person, screaming whenever she looks at someone's face, because she says that each time, she sees fearful creatures like pythons, lions, and the like. Again my old mother is with me. As a result, as I am standing here, my legs are wobbling, including my waist. I can hardly stand. Consequently, I cannot do anything, because of the stress in caring for them. I enquired of her, 'For how long has your daughter been in this state?' She answered For over five months now. Again I asked, 'And what have you been doing about it?'

She said, I invited ministers of God to pray for her, and nothing has changed.

Then I was so cross with her, not because of her problems, but because she was a member of my fellowship and she never mentioned it to me, nor did she bring it to the knowledge of any member of the fellowship.

Anyway, after rebuking her, I prayed for her and her daughter. This happened on a Friday afternoon. Three days later, as I drove through her street, I decided to call at her home to find out how she was fairing. As I walked into her compound and to my surprise I overheard her singing with joy. Thereupon, I remarked, 'Sister it is like you are well now?.' And she said to me, 'Yes, see, I have been able to do what I have not been able to do for a long time now. As I observed that, she had washed a long line of clothing, including bedspreads and. I was filled with joy and praised the Lord.

Thereafter, I enquired about her daughter and state of health. She then ushered me into flat to see her daughter. In course of my discussion with her daughter, she confirmed what her mother had told me three days earlier and how she was feeling much better then. It was clear that she regained her health after the prayer of the previous Friday afternoon.

This coincided with the day I prayed for her mother and herself in my office. Praise be to God. The point here is that Godwill always honour His Word. I am saying this to illustrate the efficacy of prayer. This simply means that there is no problem that cannot be overcome through prayer. But remember that it has to be the right Word for it to be effective. For instance, you cannot apply a healing Word if you are handling a prosperity problem. It is important that we study the Word so we can apply it appropriately. When you do this, the devil is put to flight. Jesus defeated the tempter by telling him, It is written (Matt. 4:1-10). Eve failed in the Garden of Eden because she did not remind the devil exactly what the Lord said. If you read Genesis 3:1-4, you will find the difference between what God said and what Eve told the Serpent. The Bible teaches us that God honours His Word more than even His name. The Word of God is quick and powerful, sharper than any two-edged sword; see Hebrews 4:12. Therefore, if you want a quick response from God, always remind Him of His promises.

Importance Of Being Specific

Be specific and clear in your prayers, because God does not answer ambiguous prayers. State your points clearly.

Avoid Fear Rather, Embrace Faith

Never allow the enemy to deceive you into becoming afraid, and consequently put you in a state where you would doubt God. Faith is tangible: 'Now faith is the substance of things hoped for, the evidence of things not seen" (Heb. 11:1 KJV). Therefore, hold on to it, and it will bring your miracle to pass. Again, I want you to note that faith is the opposite of fear, and fear is the weapon of the enemy, the devil; fear torments, confuses, and stresses oneout. The Word of God says 'But without faith it is impossible to please Him, for he who comes to God must believe that He is, and that He is a rewarder of those who diligently seek Him." Finally, you must be bold in your prayer and en- sure that you are in the right standing with God.

Warning!

The Devil Knows Who You Are

The enemy the devil and his demons know those who are the real children of God. Recall that the sons of Sceva according to the book of Acts, attempted to imitate Paul the Apostle in healing in the name of Jesus. God worked unusual miracles through Paul, that even the handkerchiefs or aprons brought from his body to the sick healed them and similarly evil spirits left those who were possessed. "Then some of the itinerant Jewish exorcists tried to imitate Paul by calling on of the name of the Lord Jesus to heal those who had evil spirits. They commanded: "We exorcise you by the name of Jesus whom Paul preaches..." but it did not work. In the Book of Acts 19:1-17, we gather there were seven sons of Sceva, a Jewish chief priest, who did so, and the evil spirits answered and said, 'Jesus I know, and Paul I know, but who are you?' Then the man who was possessed of the evil spirit leaped on them, overpowered and prevailed against them, and they fled out of the house naked and wounded and the name of the   Lord was magnified" (Acts 19 NKJV). This became known to all Jews and Greeks dwelling in Ephesus; and fear fell on them all and the name of the Lord was magnified. This is a great lesson to those false prophets and teachers of the Word of God. Please make sure that you do not depend on such material things as handkerchiefs as your source of spiritual power, as it could be misused and lead to negative consequences.

CHAPTER THIRTEEN

The Enemy is a Trickster

THE DEVIL IS more cunning than any other beast of the field which the Lord had created. He capitalises on the ignorance of the children of God. Ignorance, is a disease; and in law, there is a maxim which says that ignorance is no excuse, because one is punished if found guilty' you cannot plead ignorance of the law. The law must take its course. Knowledge of the Word of God is very fundamental in the life of a Christian.

No child of God can plead ignorance of the Word of God, as doing so will lead to dire consequences as was the case for Adam and Eve in the Garden of Eden. This led them to fall from grace to grass thereby bringing sufferings upon mankind.

It is important to emphasize that prayer is important in the spiritual life of a Christian. If you pray as often as you ought to and study the Word of God regularly, you will be a victorious Christian. But if you lack in any of these areas namely, prayer and knowledge of the Word, the devil will take control of you, as he did to Adam and Eve. Now let us look at what happened:

And the Lord God *commanded the man*, saying: Of every tree of the Garden you may freely eat, *But of the fruit of the tree of the knowledge of good and evil you shall not eat of it: for in the day that youeat of* it, you shall surely die, (Gen. 2:1617 NKJV).

Now you see that the instruction was quite clear and specific. Let us see how the devil twisted it and confused Eve.

And he said to the woman, Has God indeed said, "You shall *not eat of every tree* of the garden?"'

Have you observed how the devil tried to twist what the Lord said, thereby taking control of Eve and by extension, Adam! The devil often attempts to manipulate the Word of God for its own selfish purpose. From what transpired between Eve and the Devil, it is clear that Eve was ignorant of the Word of God or she may not have been aware of the injunction which God handed down to her husband. This may have been the reason why the devil went to her and not to her husband. And the woman said to the serpent, We may eat the fruit of the trees of the garden; but of the fruits of the tree which is in the midst of the garden, God said, "*You shall not eat it nor shall you touch it*, lest you die." Note here that Eve even added to what the Lord had said, as a result of her ignorance of the Lord's command to her husband, because *not eat it nor touch it* is not in God's command.

> "The serpent said to the woman, you will not surely die. "For God knows that in the day you eat of it your eyes will be opened, and you will be like God, knowing good and evil So when the woman saw that the tree was good for food, that it was pleasant to the eyes and a tree desirable to make one wise, she took of its fruit and ate. [I see a bit of pride here; she desired to be wise.] She also gave to her husband with her, and he ate." (Gen. 3:1-6 NKJV, emphasis mine)

And he ate. Oh, what a shame. The man was not in control.

This was the man to whom the Lord handed down a command not to eat of the tree of the knowledge of the good and evil; he probably did not tell his wife what the Lord commanded him to do and not to do. This should be a lesson to all men of God who have allowed their wives to manage the house without their supervision or knowledge of what happens in their houses. Another observation here was that Adam was not quite close enough to God. This was irresponsibility of the highest order.

As a matter of fact, Eve should have sought her husband's consent first, before eating of the fruit. Rather she decided to experiment by eating the fruit alone, taking advantage of her husband's indifference. We women can be very smart sometimes when a man fails to assert his spiritual authority. To crown it, Adam did not assert himself being the head of the family to whom God personally gave the command. Consequently, both of them committed sin and fell from grace. I am convinced that if Eve had really known God and His Word, she would have resisted the serpent's temptation by telling him, 'It is *written*.' Sadly, she yielded to the temptation and paid a heavy price for it.

Be Careful What You Pay Attention To

I wish also to point out that it was when the woman paid attention to the devil that she observed that the fruit was attractive and good to eat, hence the urge to eat arose in her. Never give the enemy attention, no matter how trivial or attractive a thing may seem. Remember that the enemy is manipulative, and he observes our actions all the time. He starts by dropping ideas in your mind. When he does so, compare such idea with the word of God. Ask yourself, "What does the word of God say about such situations?

May I advise women to always seek the opinion of their husbands before taking certain actions, especially in things that have to do with God.

Now food for your thought: Why did the serpent not go to the man, rather it went to the woman? The answer is quite obvious. The serpent targeted the woman because she is more vulnerable. Once a woman is worn over, the entire family is taken over. Again, I say to the women, be vigilant. His tactics have not changed; he is always attacking the families through the women. Pastors' wives, please take note and do not fail to continually pray for your husbands, no matter what they do to you, because it is possible the enemy is manipulating them.

Why did he not go to the man to whom the command was handed down? All women should be very careful and always endeavour seek the consent of their husbands before embarking on any serious project, especially when it has to do with spiritual matters. Eve failed to seek her husband's consent, and calamity was brought upon mankind.

Let me conclude by admonishing couples to ensure they always pray together. Husbands should always let their wives know what they are doing so that their wives can support them through prayer.

I say this because some men of God may think their wives are not spiritually knowledgeable enough, but they forget that the God that brought them together did so for a purpose.

When the man or the woman says 'I can do without you' or 'I can do it alone,' know that the devil is at work. Both of them must agree spiritually; the Bible tells us that one can chase a thousand and two can put ten thousand to flight. Surely, the devil is afraid of this.

Again, the Bible says that if two shall agree touching anything, it shall be done. This portion of the Bible is even more relevant when it comes to husband and wife.

CHAPTER FOURTEEN

Jesus' Prayer Format

J ESUS GAVE US ten key points of prayer format; this can be seen in the Lord's Prayer, which the Lord Jesus taught His disciples:

And it came to pass, that as he was praying in a certain place, when he ceased, one of his disciples said unto him, Lord teach us to pray, as John also taught his disciples (Luke 11:1). When the disciples of the Lord Jesus Christ asked him to teach them how to pray, he pointed them to our Lord's Prayer. This is the prayer we say every day without even pondering over its contents.

Our Father, which art in heaven, Hallowed be thy name, Thy kingdom come, Thy will be done on earth as it is in heaven. Give us this day our daily bread. And forgive us our trespasses, as we forgive those who trespass against us. Lead us not into temptation, but deliver us from evil for thine is the Kingdom, the power and the glory, Amen.

There are ten key points in the above prayer; now let us take a closer look at them.

The Ten Key Points in Our Lord's Prayer

1. Our Father which art in heaven

God was our Father before our earthly father by adoption, whom we should refer to as Abba Father: For ye have not received the spirit of bondage again to fear; but ye have received the spirit of adoption whereby ye cry Abba Father (Rom. 8:15). Some people pray to what they do not know, in the name of God. But the only God we are to pray to is our Father which is in heaven, Jehovah Elohim, the I AM THAT I AM, the Jehovah El Shaddai, the all-sufficient God, and the Father of our Lord Jesus Christ.

2. Hallowed be thy name

This means that God's name is holy, sacred, blessed, revered, venerated, honoured, sacrosanct, worshipped, and divine, and it should be treated as such with great reverence and honour. With these attributes in mind, it will help or move us to reverence God as we ought to, because He is the supreme, paramount, and only living God.

3. Thy kingdom come, Thy will be done on earth as it in heaven

It may be necessary to mention that the kingdom of God is synonymous with the kingdom of heaven as can be seen in the following passage: 'Then Jesus said to His disciples, "Assuredly, I say to you that it is hard for a rich man to enter the kingdom of heaven. And again I say to you, it is easier for a camel to go through the eye of a _ needle than fora rich man to enter the Kingdom of God' (Matt. 19:23-24 NKJV). It is therefore worthy to note that the kingdom of God and the kingdom of heaven are interchangeable, for the purpose of clarity. Here, I believe, is where God Almighty has His throne.

The kingdom of God is full of reverence, worship, holiness, and orderliness, and it is where God, the eternal creator, the Father Almighty, dwells. The kingdom of God comes into our hearts at salvation, as can be seen in the book of John: 'Jesus told Nicodemus, "Most assuredly, I say to you, unless one is born again, he cannot see the kingdom of God." He went further to say in the next vers: 'Most assuredly, I say to you, unless one is born of water and the Spirit, he cannot *enter* the kingdom of God (John 3:3, 3:5 NKJV). From the foregoing, one can say that, the first step in being born again is to begin to enjoy the goodness of God's kingdom in this world at salvation. If we honour God's name as we ought to, we will begin to enjoy the blessings of God's kingdom as we begin to do God's will in this world.

By so doing, we can bring down God's kingdom on earth. The Bible says that we are the salt and light of the world. This comes about when we live our lives as demanded in the Word of God, which includes loving our neighbours as ourselves, amid obeying God in all other areas.

4. Give us this day our daily bread

Be content with what you have today, and do not be overly anxious. But in prayer and supplication, make your request known to Him, because your heavenly Father knows your need. We are encouraged to pray to our heavenly Father daily because He knows our need. We should depend on Him and not worry.

The Bible says that we should not worry about tomorrow, because tomorrow will take care of itself: Therefore I say unto you, Take no thought for your life, what ye shall eat or what ye shall drink, noryet your body, what ye shall put on, behold the fowls of the air: for they sow not, neither do they reap, nor gather into barns; yet your heavenly Father feedeth them. Are ye not better than they? This admonishment ended by admonishing us to seek first the Kingdom of God and its righteousness, and every other thing shall be added unto us (Matt. 6:25-32). This simply means that we cannot continue our lives in sin, and at the same time expect the blessings of the Lord.

5. Forgive us our trespasses

This is a very important point. God has already forgiven us our trespasses the day we accepted Christ as our personal Lord and Saviour, like the woman caught in adultery; the Lord Jesus told her, Go and sin no more. But some people think_ that after you are born again, it doesn't matter, you can continue your life as usual. This is a lie of the devil. You are to put on the new man, which is in Christ Jesus. Be born again in your soul or spirit, through the engrafted word that is able to save your soul. This means change your ways. (.......) The Bible also says, 'Work out your salvation with fear and trembling,' (Phil. 2:12b-13). Your way of life must change. You may have to drop some of your friends, some types of movies you watch, some types of paper or magazine you read and so on; whatever will pull you down from the way of the Almighty God should be far away from you.

6. As we forgive those who trespass against us

This is an interesting part of this prayer. Many of us recite it without making it good; I mean without living it out. How many of us really forgive those who wrong us? Many of us Christians do not forgive and this constitutes hindrances to our prayers. The Word of God says if we forgive our trespassers, our Father which is in heaven will also forgive us. Most often we ignore this important admonition, forgetting that we do so at our own detriment. We cannot afford to ignore

God's Word, because God has already set out His standards for His people to follow.

7 .Lead us not into temptation

This is another important part of this prayer. Jesus warned his disciples that not praying would lead them into temptation: *Watch and pray that ye enter not into temptation"* (Matt. 26:41a KJV). You will recall that Peter fell into temptation when he denied Jesus before His crucifixion, the reason being that he didn't pray that night. Therefore, the most effective way to overcome temptation is to develop regular praying habit. To watch is to stay alive in the spirit.

8. Deliver us from evil

This is complimentary to the section 7 above. When you develop regular praying habit and live life in the spirit, evil will not come near you. Evil comes through the devil and his demons, and it is prayer that puts them to flight.

9. For thine is the kingdom

Of course, the kingdom is God's and God's only. He does not share His glory. This is why it is called God's kingdom. In the book of Revelation, the Lord said, 'I am the Alpha and the Omega, the Beginning and the End, who is and who was and who is to come, the Almighty' (Rev. 1:8 KJV).

The self-revealed God introduced Himself to Moses at Mount Horeb as the I AM, the God of Abraham, Isaac, and Jacob, I AM THAT I AM.

He is the only living God. His name is Jehovah Elohim, the self-existent God. Jehovah El Shaddai, the all-sufficient God. Before Him, there was no God, and after Him, there shall be no God. He is the Ancient of Days, the Lion of the Tribe of Judah who shares not His glory, the Man of War whose name is the LORD. We serve a great God, brethren. He is living and not dead; neither is He man-made. The kingdom is His and His only. This was what Jesus meant when He said, 'For thine is the kingdom.'

God revealed Himself to Moses at Horeb as he was tending the flock of Jethro, his father-in law, who was a priest of Midian, when he led the flock to the back of the desert: '*And the Angel of the Lord appeared to him in a flame of fire from the midst of a bush. So) he looked) and behold) the bush was burning with fire) but the bush was not consumed.*' It was at this point that Moses said to himself, '*I will now turn aside and see this great sight) why the bush does not burn.*' It was at this point that God spoke to Moses: *So when the Lord saw that he [Moses] turned aside to look, God called to him from the midst of the bush and said) Moses) Moses! And he said) 'Here I am)* (Exod. 3:3-4 KJV). I wish to point out something here: you must have observed that it was only when Moses gave his attention by turning aside that God revealed Himself to him. The lesson here is that until we give God attention, the problem which we try to solve by ourselves will be impossible to solve. Why not therefore turn it over to God, by asking Him to take over? And watch Him do the miracle for you.

10. The power and the glory

All power belongs to the Lord, and the glory is His and none other. He shares not His glory. Our God is all powerful, all knowing, all sufficient.

He is omnipotent, omniscient, and omnipresent. It is important to note that the glory of the Lord represents His power, as could be seen when the children of Israel departed from the land of Egypt. His glory followed the:i;n. When Moses went to Mount Sinai for the Ten Commandments, God's glory was seen upon him when he came down, the children of Israel could not behold his face, because of the glory of God.

God's glory was also visible when the children of Israel were removing the ark of the tabernacle from one place to the other; see Exodus 24:16-17, 16:7, 16:10, 40:34-35 respectively. As can be seen, it could also represent blessing of God as well as His anger as was the case in the wilderness when the children of Israel grumbled.

CHAPTER FIFTEEN

Various Types of Prayer

THERE ARE DIFFERENT types of prayer and the knowledge of them will be of an immense value to every believer. The aim of effective prayer is to be able to counter the enemy's plan in your life. To be victorious, over the enemy the devil, you therefore need to equip yourself with the knowledge of different kinds of prayer. The importance of acquainting yourself with such knowledge cannot be over-emphasized. If you know how to approach God and how to communicate with Him during your prayer, your request will ascend to Him faster. The Bible says, My people are destroyed for lack of knowledge (Hosea 4:6 KJV).

When you are acquainted with the knowledge of various types of prayer, such knowledge will enable you to be specific in your prayer. It will also put you in the right spiritual mood, and thus enable you communicate more effectively with God. This is important, because some prayers do not go beyond the ceilings. The following are types of prayer:

1. Prayer of petition
The word *petition* is another word for prayer or request. In this type of prayer one appeals to God to intervene and solve a particular problem.

2. Prayer of thanksgiving

In the prayer of thanksgiving, the person praying acknowledges, appreciates, or shows gratitude for what the Lord did for him or her in the past. One expresses gratitude for all the blessings of the Lord, both known and unknown blessings.

God is always doing good things for us and sometimes we may not realize it. In the Bible, He tells us: For I know the thoughts that I think toward you, saith the Lord, thoughts of peace and not of evil, to give you an expected end (future and hope, Jer. 29:11, Amp. V)

3. Prayer of worship

This is an adoration, honour, and admiration to the Lord for His supremacy, love, and care. This kind of prayer is found in the book of Psalms. King David was good at this type of prayer. You can find these in Psalms chapters 103 and 104. You can also worship God with your substance, by paying your tithe, giving to the things of God when it is called for in your church. I advise you to always give for the purpose of God's work. This is a sure source of God's blessings.

4. Prayer of praise

Like a prayer of thanksgiving, this prayer does what it says. This means to glorify and commend God for His good works upon our lives. Worshiping God through praise brings down His glory and His presence. The psalmist says that God inhabits in the praises of His people. Please be reassured that when the Lord comes, He comes with revelations and blessing. Therefore, always endeavour to bring down God's presence in or during your prayer by going into praises.

5. Prayer of intercession

Intercession means to intercede, mediate, or intervene on behalf of another or others. It means standing in for others or someone who needs divine intervention. The Holy Spirit also intercedes on our behalf: *Likewise the Spirit also helpeth our infirmities: for we know not what we should pray for as we ought: But the Spirit itself maketh intercession for us with groanings which cannot be uttered* (Rom. 8:26 KJV). In the Bible, Timothy was told among other things to exhort that intercession be made for the saints; that is, encourage the congregation to make intercession for others: *Exhort therefore that) first of all) supplications) prayers) intercessions) and giving of thanks) be made for all men* (1 Tim. 2:1 KJV). Jesus also made intercession for sinners, *He was numbered with the transgressors; and He bare the sins of many and made intercession for the transgressors* (Isa. 53:12b KJV). He still makes intercession for us because He is sitting at the right hand of His Father.

6. Prayer of warfare

Spiritual warfare is what the Christian race is all about. In the book of Ephesians, we are admonished to be strong in the Lord and in the power of His might: *'Finally) my brethren) be strong in the Lord and in the power of His might. Put on the whole armour of God) that ye may be able to stand against the wiles of the devil. For we wrestle not against flesh and blood) but against powers) against the rulers of darkness of this world) against spiritual wickedness in high places. Wherefore take unto you the whole armour of God'* (Eph. 6:10-18 KJV). Armour in this context means spiritual arms not firearms. You will find below types of armour and what they represent:

I. Truth - on your loins **(honesty)**
II. Righteousness your breastplate
   (protection for your salvation)
III. Preparation of the gospel of peace
   (protection for your feet)
IV. Faith - a shield **(protection for your heart)**
V. Salvation - your helmet **(ensures your access into heaven)**
VI. The word of God **(the sword of the spirit)**
VII. Prayer **(for your spiritual well-being)**

The list above shows that there are other things we need to take care of in addition to prayer, so that our prayer can be effective. We must live out our Christian life so all who know us will bear witness that we are children of God. Jesus admonished us thus: *'Let your light so shine before men, that they may see your good works and glorify your Father which is in Heaven.'* Let me tell you a short story concerning, the preparation of the gospel of peace. There was a sister in my church some years ago, whom I had not seen in the church for sometime. When I eventually saw her, she had developed a big sore which got her leg swollen, broken, and was sore, it was a very pathetic sight. I enquired from her why she was in such a sorry state, and she told me that the injury started in a small way until it became big. Immediately the Holy Spirit cut in and said to me, *Tell her to go and carry out evangelism.'*

In the process of delivering the message to her, she confirmed by saying, Yes, my sister, , I used to do it but I suddenly stopped. The anointing is so much on me that whenever I wash my clothes and spread, smoke comes out of them. Again, people were giving their lives to Christ just in droves. Brethren, needless to say that this sister is highly anointed. But she was hiding her anointing; consequently, she was not affecting those that she was meant to affect with her anointing. The Lord dislikes such attitude. But you do not have to be so anointed in order to affect people's lives around you spiritually; The Bible says that he that wins a soul is wise. Again this story confirms the fact that witnessing or evangelism is a weapon against the enemy, as well as a source of blessing to us. Therefore, brethren, go out and tell someone the good news of salvation.

8. Prayer of supplication

This type of prayer is an intense pleading, after every other thing has failed. This is the kind of prayer which Jesus described as importunity in the book of Luke, the type the widow made to a judge that feared neither God nor man:

> There was in a city, a judge who feared not God, neither regarded man. And there was a widow in that city; and she came unto him saying, Avenge me of my adversary. And he would not for a while, but afterward he said within himself, Though I fear not God, nor regard man; yet because this widow troubleth me, I will avenge her, lest by her continual coming she weary me. And Jesus said, shall not God avenge his own elect, which cry day and night unto him ... I tell you that He will avenge them speedily. (Luke 18:1-8 KJV)

This is a steadfast and consistent prayer to God, the type that Daniel and Hannah, the mother of Samuel, made. Daniel's prayer was hindered but because of his persistence, an angel was dispatched to deliver the answer to him. Hannah received an answer instantly and, before long, gave birth to Samuel the prophet who affected people's lives and was a great man of God, (1Sam. 1and 2).

9. Prayer of travail

The word travail is to wail in pains like a woman in labour, It is like the type of prayer our Lord Jesus prayed in the Garden of Gethsemane, before His crucifixion. A travailing prayer is an agonizing prayer - after you might have been or accused falsely. This will move you to travail in prayer. This type of prayer will move you to toil, roll, and wail on the floor.

10. Prayer of binding and loosing

The prayer of binding and loosing is a very powerful prayer that can send the demons out of your prayer arena before you start praying. It can also be applied elsewhere. For instance, this type of prayer can be applied in your family, business place, office, marriage, finance, and so on. Having cast out the demons you must cast them into a particular domain, like dry places, wilderness. Recall that when the Lord Jesus cast demons out of the lunatic who lived in the tomb, the demons begged Him to cast them into the swine, and as soon as He did, the swine ran violently into the deep Matt. 8:28-32

You should also remember that demons behave like flies. They do not go away for too long, but will always return, therefore always fill the vacuum with the Word of God, by telling Him to take control of all your mind; also cover yourself with the Blood of Jesus. Therefore, you will need to be sensitive in the spirit in order to know when they are operating around you. In effect you should always be steadfast and consistent in prayer.

Jesus released the power to bind and loose to us, through Peter as recorded in the Gospel of Matthew. In response to Peter's reply as to who people thought Jesus Christ was, Jesus said, Blessed art thou, Simon Bar-jona: for flesh and blood hath not revealed it unto thee, but my Father which is in heaven . . . And I will give unto thee the keys of the Kingdom of heaven: and whatever thou shalt bind on earth shall be bound in heaven: and whatever thou shalt loose on earth shall be loosed in heaven. (Matt. 16:13-19 KJV)

The ability to bind and cast is very important, and it is the key to the kingdom of heaven.

No wonder some people, especially the devil's agents, are always afraid of this type of prayer; it is powerful. You can also loose your blessings_ and whatever else you would want to loose, and call upon the angels of the Lord to surround you during and after your prayer. Remember this prayer will need to be reactivated repeatedly by reminding the angels of the Lord, as I have already mentioned above.

Healing By Casting Out Demons

Jesus says, No man can enter into a strong man's house and spoil his goods except he will first bind the strong man: and then he will spoil his house (Mark 3:1-11, 3:23-27 NKJV). Jesus made this assertion after he had cast out demons from the possessed man, thereafter the Pharisees accused Him of violating the Sabbath instead of being appreciative. I find it rather awful that some people do not appreciate good works. In such a situation, what should you do? Ignore them, of course, and carry on.

11. Prayer of agreement

A prayer of agreement is a very powerful prayer; it is the kind of prayer every husband and wife should be praying. It has really helped my marriage; the testimonies are enormous. This is why congregational prayers are very effective.

The Bible highly recommends it: Again I say unto you that if two of you shall agree on earth as touching anything that they shall ask, it shall be done for them of my Father which is in heaven (Matt. 18:19 KJV). Again, the Word of God says that one can chase a thousand and two can chase ten thousand. The way I work this out is, for every one person in the group, you add one zero (0) at the end of the figure. In case you do not understand, I mean if one can chase one thousand (1,000) and two can chase ten thousand (10,000), it follows that three persons will chase one hundred thousand (100,000).

This can simply be arrived at by adding one zero to the last zero. This may seem unbelievable, but I can tell you that I have worked it out by the wisdom from the Holy Ghost. Let me break it down below:

1 person = 1,000
2 persons = 10,000
3 persons = 100,000 and so on.

Imagine therefore when a congregation prays, it can be very powerful. Recall when Paul and Silas prayed in the prison and the Holy Ghost came down and the angels of the Lord loosened the chains from their feet and hands; the power of God manifested itself. The guards who were detailed to watch over them were frightened and attempted to commit suicide. In the case of Peter, the guard repented and became a follower of Christ without being ministered to. It was indeed_ remarkable - the power of prayer.

12. Prayer of faith

In a prayer of faith, you exercise your faith through belief in God based on His promises as expressed in His Word. And the Bible says whatever we need, when we pray, we should believe that we have received it and so it shall be unto us. The Word of God also tells us that, "Whatever is not of faith is sin. Therefore, to receive from God we must exercise our faith in Him. For without faith it is impossible to please Him: for he that cometh to God must believe that He is, and that He is a rewarder of those who diligently seek Him (Heb. 11:6 KJV).

13. Prayer of dedication

To dedicate is to hand over something precious to someone for safekeeping. In a prayer of dedication, you are handing over something to God for safekeeping. This is why it is important to dedicate your children to God. You could also dedicate yourself, your marriage, your house or houses, landed properties, and so on. If you are not sure your parents dedicated you to God, you surrender yourself for dedication through your pastor who has to be a born-again man of God, to dedicate you to God. It is better late than never.

14. Prayer of repentance

We all know what repentance is. For those who do not know, it means turning away from your old ways. In this type of prayer, confession comes first and is followed by a promise to repent from whatever sin. It could be sin of omission or commission. One can commit sin by failing to do what one should have done or do something which one should not have done.

15. Prayer of confession

Confession is very important in a believer's life. A former occultist revealed that Christians who do not confess their sins are more prone to spiritual attack than those who regularly confess their sins. This does not mean that we should be living in sin, because the Bible says that our righteousness is like a filthy rag. This type of prayer can be said on personal, congregational, community, and even at national levels. The same goes for the prayer of repentance.

16. Corporate prayer

This type of prayer is a very powerful prayer, because it involves many worshippers, and induces corporate anointing. This type of anointing is common in churches, fellowships, and other religious gatherings.

17. Prophetic prayer action

Prophetic action takes place during an intensive prayer. Here the Holy Spirit is in control, telling you what to do or say. This type again comes with great anointing; it should not be faked. Any prayer under prophetic action is usually very effective because you are praying the mind of God. The Holy Ghost may urge you to draw a battle line in the case of someone challenging you and. I say this based on my experience.

18. Prophetic prayer

This type of prayer as stated above, is influenced by prophetic utterances during an intensive prayer. Usually, the Holy Spirit puts words and unction in your spirit.

I had a neighbour who was an occultist, and I did not know it; The devil tried to use her to torment me and so one morning, she came to my gate to lure me into a fight, by forcing my gate open and making a lot of noise. She claimed that my prayer was disturbing her and her group. Then members of her Satanic group sent her to come and confront me. Of course, I ignored her because the Lord had revealed her to me, and so one day, as I prayed, the Holy Ghost said to me, 'Draw a battle line.' This I did, and the Lord began to give me prayer utterances. Barely a week after that prayer, she was forcibly evicted from the house. I said 'the house' because the abode did not belong to her; she and her Satanic group merely wanted to use it as a base for their evil operations, and a base through which they could attack me.

One day she went out, and on her return, she found, to her dismay, that her belongings had been thrown outside under the rain. This is how effective a prophetic prayer can be. But you have to be sure it is being directed by the Lord.

19. Prophetic intercession

Again, this type of prayer comes from the Holy Spirit. It comes as an urge to pray for someone, a nation, even a situation you had no knowledge of. God can lead you to intercede for someone God once led me to pray for a relation who lived about a hundred miles away. I did not know what her problem was, but I prayed generally for her well-being. I decided to pray in tongues since I did not know what her problem was. When I saw her about a month after, I enquired if she had any problem about a month earlier, and surprisingly, she told me that she was sick and nearly died. On reflection I thanked God that I obeyed Him and prayed. That was a prophetic intercession because God directed me to do it.

20. Tongue praying

Tongue praying is a heavenly kind of prayer, because you are speaking the language of the Holy Spirit. He gives one the utterance, and sometimes you could interpret if He so desires. However, it is important for everyone who speak in tongues to pray for ability to interpret the tongue. But if the Holy Spirit wishes to keep it secret from you, depending on the content of the tongue, He may not give you the interpretation. The reason being probably, to prevent you from giving out the information, or getting frightened if the revelation is not a good one. The Lord reveals evil to His children if He wants you to pray against it or to go and warn someone, as per the Lord's admonition in the book of Ezekiel.

CHAPTER SIXTEEN

Who Should Pray?

THE BIBLE SAYS that the effectual or specific prayer of a believer is very effective. After you have given your life to Christ, the angels are always anxiously waiting to pass your prayer to the throne room of God: The *effectual fervent* prayer of the righteous availeth much (James 5:16b KJV). This goes to explain why the prayer of an unbeliever is hardly answered. It is the grace of God that keeps the non-believer going. Holy living also opens the way to God very fast. By this, I mean being obedient to the word of God, or God's command. Being specific in whatever you want God to do for you is important, because God does not answer an ambiguous prayer.

Now let us examine the following terms: look at these terms: *effectual, fervent, prayer, and the righteous* and what they really mean.

Effectual: This means effective, productive, successful, constructive, efficacious, and worthwhile prayer.

Fervent: Intent, passionate, vehement, ardent, sincere, heartfelt, enthusiastic, zealous, fanatical, eager, keen, committed, and dedicated. During fervent prayer,

God may reveal information to us as we convey our emotion or feeling to Him.

Prayer: Prayer is a form of communication,_ and in communication, we share and exchange information; It involves two beings, and in this case, you and God. In other words, prayer involves a relationship. There must be a relationship between you and God.

The righteous: No one can claim to be righteous based on his or her works. The Lord Jesus is our righteousness and the righteous therefore is the one who has accepted the Lord Jesus Christ as one's personal Lord and Saviour, through the exercise of one's faith on Christ who died for us. The person who does the will of God is the one acceptable to Him.

The Bible tells us to love our neighbour as ourselves, and Jesus used the example of the story of the Good Samaritan to drive this home. In this story a lawyer wanted to justify himself, when he asked Jesus, Who is my neighbour? And Jesus told him the story of the Good Samaritan in the book of Luke, (Luke 10:25-37). This is the type of person whose prayer avails much.

Certainty Of Answered Prayer

Jesus says in the book of Mark 11, when you pray, believe. This means that even when our prayer has not yet been answered, we should believe that God has heard us, without doubting in our mind. Exercise your faith and be patient with God. Remember that

Faith is the substance of things hoped for, the evidence of things not seen (Heb. 11:1). Again Jesus has given us assurance when He said: And I say unto you, Ask, and it shall be given unto you; seek, and ye shall find; knock, and it shall be opened unto you. For every one that asketh receiveth; and he that seeketh findeth; and to him that knocketh it shall be opened" (Luke 11:9-10 KJV). Furthermore, He assured us that before we ask it shall be answered.

Prayer Of The Wicked

The Bible says, 'The sacrifice of the wicked is an abomination to the Lord, but the prayer of the upright is his delight.' In effect, "The Lord is far from the wicked; but he hears the prayer of the righteous" (Prov. 15:8, 15:29 KJV). Remember that anyone without Christ is considered as wicked. You may ask, 'Why?' It is very simple; without Christ, one cannot live a sinless life, because it is Christ that gives us the enablement to live a sinless life, through His Holy Spirit.

Your prayer can help change situations in your family, community, and even your nation. Today, there is a non-denominational Fellowship in my community as I am writing this book, where the entire membership and all the churches in the community gather to pray on a monthly basis. And the Lord is using it to do a great exploit in the land. Souls are being saved, churches are being filled, and people are being affected positively.

Ministers who never knew about the concept of being born again are now understanding and are applying it in their churches, and thereby affect their congregations positively. As you pray, the Lord will do the same in your community.

The Bible admonishes us to pray for those in authority, and they include national leaders, church leaders, leaders of all the essential establishments in your nation.

See what Austin Phelps said about the prayer of a sinner in contrast to that of a righteous (saved) person.

Your heart has to be right with God, for you to enjoy the presence of God. He went further to say,

If the heart is not right with God, enjoyment of communion with God is impossible. That communion itself is impossible (...)the impenitent sinner never prays. Impenitence involves not one of the elements of a spirit of prayer. Holy desire, holy love, holy fear, holy trust, not one of these can the sinner find within himself. He has therefore none of the artless spontaneity, in calling upon God, which David exhibited when he said: 'Thy servant hath found in his heart to pray this prayer unto thee.' An impenitent sinner finds no such thing in his heart. He finds there is no intelligent wish to enjoy God's friendship. The whole atmosphere of prayer, therefore is foreign to his tastes. If he drives himself into it for a time, by forcing upon his soul the form of devotion, he cannot stay there. He is like one gasping in a vacuum.

He Went Further To Say:

The notes of a flute are sometimes a torture to the ears of the mentally impaired, like the blare of a trumpet. The reason has been conjectured to be the melodious sound unlock the tomb of the impaired mind by the suggestion of conceptions, dim, but startling; like a revelation of a higher life, with which that mind has certain crushed affinities, but with which it feels no willing sympathy; so that its own degradation, disclosed to it by the contrast, it seated upon the consciousness of the mentally impaired like a nightmare. Such a stimulant only to suffering, may the form of prayer be in the experience of sin. Impenitent prayer can only grovel in stagnant sensibility, or agonize in remorseful torture, or oscillate from one to the other. There is no point of joy between, to which it can gravitate and there rest.

It is not wise that even we who profess to be followers of Christ, should close our eyes to this truth, that the uniform absence of joy in prayer is one of the threatening signs in respect of our religious state. It is one of the legitimate intimations of that estrangement from God, which sin induces in one who has not experienced God's renewing grace.

There are differences when a sinner and a righteous (saved) person pray. The saved person enjoys the presence of God in his or her prayer, but the unsaved person struggles in his or her prayer, because he or she does not enjoy the presence of God; hence, the prayer of the unsaved person is hardly answered. Let us take a look at a few examples from Austin Phelps:

Austin Phelps had these to say about a prayer of the unsaved:

"Bishop Hall, in uttering this lament, two and a half centuries ago, only echoed the wail which had come down through living hearts from the patriarchs, whose story is the oldest known literature in any language. A consciousness of the absence of God is one of the standard incidents of religious life. Even when the forms of devotion are observed conscientiously, the sense of the presence of God, as an invisible friend, whose society is a joy, is by no means unintermittent. The truth of this will not be questioned by one who is familiar with those phrases of religious experience which are so often the burden of Christian confession. In no single feature of 'inner life,' probably, is the experience of many minds less satisfactory to them than in this. They seem to themselves in prayer, to have little, if any, effluent emotion. They can speak of little devotional life that seem to them like life; of little that appears like the communion of a living soul with a living God. Are there not many 'closet hours' in which the chief feeling of the worshipper is an expressed consciousness of the absence of reality from his own exercise? He has no words which are, as George Herbert says, 'heart deep.' He not only experiences no ecstasy, but no joy, no peace, no repose. He has no sense of being at home with God. The stillness of the hour is the stillness of a dead calm at sea. They hear rocks monotonously on the surface of the great thoughts of God, of Christ, of Eternity and of Heaven -

a) **'As idle as a painted ship**
b) **Upon a painted ocean.'**

Such experiences in prayer are often startling, in the contrast with those of certain Christians, whose communion with God, as the hints of it are recorded in their biographies, seems to realise, in actual being, the scriptural conception of a life which is hid with Christ in God.

We read of Payson, that his mind, at times, almost lost the sense of the external world, in the ineffable thoughts of God's glory, which rolled of light around him, at the throne of grace.

We read of Cowper, that, in one of the few lucid hours of his religious life, such was the experience of God's presence which he enjoyed in prayer, that, as he tells us, he thought he should have died with joy, if special strength had not been imparted to him to bear the disclosure.

We read of one of the Tennents, that on one occasion, when he was engaged in secret devotion, so overpowering was the revelation of God which opened upon his soul, and with augmenting intensity of refulgence as he prayed, that at length he recoiled from the intolerable joy as from a pain, and besought God to withhold from him further manifestations of His glory. He said, 'Shall Thy servant see Thee and live?'

We read of the 'sweet hours' which Edwards enjoyed 'on the banks of Hudson's River, in secret converse with God,' and hear his own description of the inward sense of Christ which at times came into his heart, and which he 'knows not how to express otherwise than by a calm, sweet abstraction of soul from all the concern of this world; and sometimes a kind of vision . . . of being alone in the mountains, or some solitary wilderness, far from all mankind, sweetly conversing with Christ, and rapt and swallowed up in God.'

We read of such instances of the fruits of prayer, in the blessedness of the suppliant, and are we reminded by them of transfiguration of our Lord, of whom we read, 'As he prayed, the fashion of his countenance was altered, and his raiment became white and glistering'? Who of us is oppressed by the contrast between such an experience and his own? Does not the cry of the patriarch come unbidden to our lips, 'Oh that I knew where I might find Him'? (Austin Phelps, *Communion with God*)

The above narratives remind me of my many wonderful experiences in the presence of God, some of which time will not permit me to write down here. But I must mention this particular experience when the

Lord came to save me in a theatre room during surgery, during which I found myself worshiping there with the Lord Jesus in a garden so well lit with different colourful light bulbs; and there was Jesus, who came to rescue me from the sting of death. It was such a serene atmosphere, such a wonderful experience that, when I finally came out of the anaesthetic influence, I found myself on the floor of the theatre, singing the very worship song that I was singing with the Lord in that garden. I desired to go back to continue in the worship.

Another one was in 1981, after I gave birth to my daughter. I got admitted into the hospital, and eventually went into a coma for many days; the news had it that I was dead, but the Lord again showed up. One night, while I was still in coma, I found myself sitting in a market square, in what I would call a dream, but the market was empty. I was the only one sitting there, and a young handsome gentleman whom I believed was the Lord Jesus Christ or an angel, came to me, and said, 'Madam, I have come to bring you hosanna,' which was interpreted to me to mean 'healing', though there are other meanings assigned to this word, for instance: an exclamation of praise, blessing, and salvation, which people shouted during Jesus' triumphant entry into Jerusalem; (Matt. 21:9 Mark 11:9 John 12:13), but 'healing' was what the Holy Spirit impressed upon my spirit for my situation, and I said to him, 'Thank you', and repeated the word *hosanna* immediately. I woke up from the coma healed and was instantly discharged. Like

I said earlier, time would not permit me to write down here all my experiences with the Lord Jesus Christ, and it is still ongoing, praise God.

Even on my knees when I am praying, it is usually as though the Lord is seated upon a chair by my side, chatting with me. It is usually an experience which I can hardly express here. It is usually filled with such glorious feeling of ecstasy, beyond rational thought and self-control a great peaceful atmosphere surrounded by illumination.

I wish to stress here that this experience is not peculiar to some special people; it is promised to as many as believe on His name (see Mark 16:1518). You may read a little more on the testimonies sections.

There Is Power In The Prayer Of The Righteous

Developing a persistent prayer life is a sure way_ to defeat the enemy, in other words, you will need to be a fanatical Christian. The word 'fanatic' is no doubt a taboo to some people. This word simply means to possess an excessive zeal for whatever one believes in. This is what Jesus demands from His followers. In the book of Revelation, Jesus warned the Church of the Laodiceans the danger in being lukewarm, that is being neither hot nor cold: ..«*J know thy works, that thou art neither hot nor cold: I would that thou were cold or hot. So then because thou art lukewarm, and neither cold nor hot, I will spew thee out of my mouth,* (Rev. 3:14-

16, KJV). Jesus therefore prefers His followers to be up and doing and not be passive. Hence fanaticism is an appropriate adjective for a committed Christian.

The power of God is present in every committed and righteous Christian. This is made manifest in the books of Matthew, Luke, and Mark. When Jesus sent His twelve disciples out and said to them: "The Kingdom of heaven is at hand·. Heal the sick, cleanse the lepers, raise the dead, cast out devils: freely ye have received, freely give, (Mtt. 10:6-8; Luke 9:3-5; Mark 16:15, KJV).

CHAPTER SEVENTEEN

Things That Can Hinder Your Prayer

I T IS NOT everyone's prayer that are answered. Some people's prayers are hindered for various reasons, some of these reasons are unconfessed sins; lack of forgiveness; and disobedience to God's commands in general. God views confession of sins very seriously, because He is a righteous God who cannot behold iniquities. One should not hide one's sins or pretend to be sinless. The Word of God makes us to know that he who says he has no sins makes God a liar. Again he who denies that Jesus is the Christ is a liar and antichrist, (1John 2).

Hear what a repentant occult grandmaster in his book Occult Grand Master Turns to Christ said: **when believers do not confess their sins during their bedtime prayers, they are vulnerable to spiritual attacks, and this was how we were able to attack them in their sleep**.' The Bible says we should confess our sins one to another. This means you can confess your sins to a fellow believer. Remember that this doesn't mean one should dwell in sin. Once you confess your sins please forsake them. Jesus told the woman caught in adultery to 'Go and sin no _ more.' I cannot overemphasize the fact that sin hinders our prayers from being answered.

A major and very basic one is refusal to accept the Son of God, the Lord Jesus Christ, as one's personal Lord and Saviour. Accepting the Lord Jesus Christ as one's personal Lord and Saviour is a powerful tool against the enemy, because by this Jesus' righteousness would have been imputed into you. Please read the book of Romans chapter 8 very regularly, this will help your spiritual growth.

Who Should Pray?

Most people pray but it is not everyone's prayer that ascends to God, for various reasons. Firstly, the prayers of those who do not have relationship with the Lord Jesus do not ascend to God. For one to be able to achieve results, one must be in the right standing with the Lord Jesus Christ. Second are those who do not confess their sins. The third group are those who deliberately continue in sin.

The Bible says that the prayer of the wicked is an abomination to the Lord, but the prayer of the upright is His delight, (Prov. 15:8).

Again, the Bible says that the wicked is an abomination unto the Lord, but He loveth him that followeth after righteousness (Prov. 15:9). It is necessary to know who the Bible refers to as the wicked. The wicked is the unjust, or unrighteous person. God does not condone unrighteousness; He enjoins us to work before Him and be perfect for He is perfect. You may ask: 'Who can be as perfect as Him?' The Bible tells us that our righteousness is of the Lord. This means that Jesus is our righteousness. All we need to do is to exercise faith in His atonement death on the cross of Calvary. Repent, invite Him into your life, and be saved.

Forgiveness Is A Weapon

Forgiving someone who has offended you is a powerful weapon against the enemy, it opens the way to where God dwells. Hear what the Bible says about it: 'For if you forgive men their trespasses, your heavenly Father will also forgive you. But if you do not forgive men their trespasses, neither will your Father forgive you of your trespasses' (Matt. 6:14-15 KJV). Again the Bible says, before you come to the presence of God or God's altar, you should have your offering, but if you remember that you had a problem with your brother (this could be anybody), then you should leave your offering at the altar and go to make up with your brother; this is simply referring to forgiveness. Jesus is the final sacrifice; this_ is why it is important that you give your life to Christ.

Be Violent In The Spirit

In his book, *Prayer That Moves Mountains*, Gordon Lindsay says that, "everyone should pray a violent prayer every day. And the Bible makes us understand that right from the time of John the Baptist, the kingdom of Heaven suffereth violence and the violent taketh it by force (Matt. 11:12). Note that violence here is not referring to physical violence. Therefore, do not engage your neighbour in physical combat, but what the Bible recommends is being fervent and steadfast in your prayer.

CHAPTER EIGHTEEN

Fasting

FASTING IS VERY essential in the life of a Christian; without fasting, it will be impossible to excel spiritually. Jesus always fasted even before He started His ministry; every Christian should therefore emulate Him. If Jesus who was God but came into this world in human flesh could fast, how much more mere mortals like us?

Fasting is not just abstinence from food, but a time for solemn prayer and repentance. It is the time we set aside to cry out unto our God, as well as fellowship with Him. Any fasting that focuses only on abstinence from food without prayer is meaningless. The importance of fasting in the life of a believer cannot be overemphasised. Fasting acts as fuel in a believer's spiritual life, because it takes one to a higher spiritual realm.

Pastor J entezen Franklin in his book 'fasting' refers to fasting as dethroning king stomach.' "fasting means crucifying what I refer to as King Stomach." And in case you don't know who King Stomach is, just move this book out of the way, look down, and introduce yourself.

You have probably already heard him rumble in disagreement a time or two since you began reading this book," referring to his book. Making reference to King

Solomon's book of wisdom, he referred to fasting as one of the threefold cord, (giving, praying, and fasting) which is not easily broken. It is therefore worthy to note that fasting alone may not be able to solve all your problems. Fasting energizes one and spurs one-up to pray more intensely. It lifts one higher into the spirit realm and helps one to pray more effectively and fervently. It also helps us to receive from the Holy Spirit, and this way we can ensure we are praying in line with the will of God, thus we achieve a breakthrough in our prayers. The Bible teaches us to understand that a carnal man cannot please God and is in fact, an enemy of God. If you are ignorant of the Word of God, you can be sure you are carnal and barren spiritually, and. therefore cannot please God, much less talk of receiving from Him.

Study To Show Yourself Approved

The Bible enjoins us to study the Bible in order to be approved by God and not to be ashamed to work with God, "Study to shew yourself approved unto God, a workman that needed not to be ashamed, rightly dividing the Word of truth," (2Tim. 2:15 KJV). Now let us see how New King James' Version puts it: "Be diligent to present yourself approved to God, a worker who does not need to be ashamed, rightly dividing the Word of truth," (2Tim. 2:15 NKJV). This simply means that every Christian should always read and study the

Bible. Because once you tell someone that you are born again, they will surely bombard you with questions, and you will need to know what you are saying in order to be able to give a convincing answer. You cannot give out what you don't have.

Again, we are admonished in another passage to meditate on the Word of God day and night: "This book of the law shall not depart out of your mouth, but you shall meditate in it day and night, that you may observe to do according to all that is written in it. For then you will make your way prosperous, and then you will have good success (Josh. 1:8 NKJV). It is not possible to meditate on something you do not know; therefore, endeavour to have the Word of God in your heart so that you will be able to tell the devil, 'It is written', that is, quote the Bible to the devil.' This comes only through studying the Bible daily.

Jesus' Encounter With The Devil

Immediately after Jesus was baptized, He went first into fasting, and after the fast, the Spirit of God led Him into the wilderness to be tempted. He emerged victorious because He had fasted. Thereafter, He was filled with the Holy Spirit and was able to tell the devil, 'It is written.' This confirms the fact that fasting helps a believer to live a victorious Christian life, no matter your rank, office, or spiritual level.

What To Watch Before You Embark On Your Fast

The Lord says in His Word that we should do everything with wisdom. It is therefore necessary to check ourselves before we embark on fasting. Things to consider may include one's health. and mood. In other words, one's body, soul, and spirit must be in agreement.

A sick person may not be able to embark on an effective fasting. And the same goes for an a:hgry or emotionally disturbed person, for instance a bereaved or traumatized person. Anyone who falls in any of the above-mentioned categories may not be able to embark on an effective fast, because it is fruitless to embark on a fast half-heartedly. Let me add that anyone taking prescription drugs or medication, is advised to complete such prescription drugs before embarking on a fast.

Bow To Overcome The Devil During Your Fast

The devil will always want to hinder you from fasting. Therefore, you must endeavour to confront him and put him to flight before you start the fast. Ask the Lord for divine strength. To keep the devil away, you must replace fear with faith. Fear is a major weapon of the enemy. He will use it to keep you away from fasting, because he knows that your fasting will ensure your victory. Therefore, replace fear with faith, for without faith it is impossible to please God. Your prayer do not need to be audible for God to hear. You can pray silently in your mind and your prayer will be equally effective as much as the verbal one as long as you pray in faith.

In your mind you can bind the devil, and the angels will carry out your commands. Do not allow yourself to be intimidated in any way, because the devil is always very subtle.

Bringing Down The Power Of God, During Your Fast

The Bible tells us that God inhabits in the praises of His children; therefore, you should start your prayer by worshiping and praising God.

If you try this method, you will find your prayer very . . .

Keep The Devil Running

God gave me a song which puts the devil to flight whenever I am fasting, because the devil will always attempt to weaken you spiritually with hunger. The lyrics of the son goes like this:

Satan, get behind me x3
Man shall not live by bread alone

You can apply your own tune, and I assure you that this song will send the devil to flight instantly, because it is the Word of God which the Lord Jesus invoked to defeat the devil in the wilderness.

Fasting Tips:

1. Drink plenty of water before and during the fast drink if you feel thirsty
2. Pray for the Lord to strengthen you
3. Write out your prayer-points

Fasting for Beginners

If you have not fasted before, start with a few hours, say for instance, 6 a.m.9 a.m. or 6 a.m.-12 noon etc, and gradually you can go to 6 a.m.-6 p.m. This way, you'll find fasting very easy. Please drink water a lot of water, it will help to wash away toxins from your system and keep you from being dehydrated.

The first day is always hard, but as you persist, it becomes a part of you, then you will start experiencing victory in your Christian life and even feeling healthier.

Remember what Jesus said to His disciples, 'This type goeth not away but by fasting and prayer.' This means that there are certain problems in your life which will require fasting in addition to prayer. As you continue in your fasting and as you begin to experience breakthroughs, you may not want to discontinue. Some problems may require one day's fast, some three, some seven, and some more, as the Spirit of God leads you.

Help from Above

If you are someone who is always afraid of fasting, what you need to do is to pray to God to help you before you embark on the fast; this way, you will receive help surely and immediately, in the form of strength from above. This approach works because the Lord always appreciates His children when they fast.

You need the Holy Spirit

The Holy Spirit is your helper. Jesus sent us the Holy Spirit in order that He might help us. This is why He is called a helper'. Invite Him to help you. The Bible encourages us to ask, seek, and knock.

CHAPTER NINETEEN

Applying Prophetic Actions

Pacing

THE ACTIONS WE take during our prayer are important; for instance, we kneel down to show respect and humility towards our Creator. Therefore, when you pray in the spirit and the Spirit of God moves you to stand up and pace up and down, this signifies a battle in the spiritual; when this happens, the Holy Spirit is usually in control, and you are supposed to yield to His leading. It usually involves confronting the devil or his demons, because the enemy operates through his demons. You cannot defeat your enemy by retreating but by confronting them; hence, the Holy Spirit will move you to pace up and down, putting you in the mood for a battle.

Turn Your Face Against Them

This action may also involve turning your face against the enemy prophetically; this means rejecting all his moves, plans, suggestions, and operations by speaking out battle language which will be given to you by the Holy Spirit. Because the enemy cannot stand confrontation.

Fire of the Holy Ghost

Release the fire of the Holy Ghost at the demons who are carrying out operations against you by speaking the Word into the atmosphere against them. Remember this may be why the Lord Jesus baptized us with fire; this is a powerful prayer language, and it is effective. One day, I was praying, and there was a neighbour who is involved in witchcraft; each time, she channelled her evil operations towards me. And of course, I would always be at war with this witchcraft spirit. As I persisted, I discovered that my prayer was affecting her, and she was not as active as she used to be; as I wondered, the Lord asked, 'Don't you know that all the fire you have been kindling has been burning her?" And I praised God. You can also release the fire of the Holy Ghost at the demons in operation within the area you are located, including the entire environment around you. God might have placed you there as a territorial leader. You should be in control of the entire territory spiritually. Jesus said, 'Occupy till I come.' This is not just a physical occupation but a spiritual occupation. You are the territorial power for God in that area. You will need to fortify yourself spiritually by constantly being in the spirit through prayer and occasionally embarking on a fast on your own and as the Spirit of God leads you, because the enemy will surely target you. But be not afraid, for God is on your side and has made all the spiritual weapons available for you Greater is he that is with us than he that is in the world (lJohn 4:4b KJV).

Applying Prophetic Actions

Fear and the Dread of God

I wish to remind you again that the angels are waiting for you to release a spiritual command for them to work with, and once you do, they will use it to go to work in your favour. So release the fear and dread of God upon the demons in operation, and they will flee; remember when you pray, believe, not mixing it with doubt or fear.

Witches and Wizards:

These are people who can bewitch or cast a spell on someone. They are sorcerers and enchanters, and operate through familiar and occult spirits; they also use mediums in their operations. They are also referred to as follows: charmers, consulters with familiar spirits, or necromancers (Deut. 18:11).

The same medium might seek both types of demons, namely, one who consults a familiar spirit and a knowing spirit. They bring up spirits _ which impersonate a dead relation, a friend, depending on the desire of their client.

Let us see what the Bible says about those who consult witches and wizards: Manasseh made his sons pass through the fire and observed times, used enchantments, and dealt with familiar spirits and wizards; he wrought much wickedness in the sight of the Lord. A a result of his wickedness, the servants of

Amon, his son, conspired and slew him in his house (2 Kings 21:22-23).

The Bible lets us know that Saul consulted one who pretended to have invoked Samuel's spirit from the grave.

> And Saul disguised himself and put on other raiment, and he went, and two men with him, and they came to the woman by night: and he said, I pray thee divine unto me by the familiar spirit, and bring him up, whom I shall name unto thee. (1 Sam. 28:8 -11 KJV).

If you read further, you will find that the woman (the sorcerer) invoked Samuel's spirit. You should not be afraid of them, because this is the ultimate goal of the devil, to make you afraid in order for him to torment you, and consequently suggest to you a sinful way out.

In case you find yourself becoming afraid of them, remember that God is with you, because you are carrying God, Jesus, and the Holy Spirit inside you. He that is in you is greater than he that is in the world (1st John 4:4, KJV). Again, he that is with God is with majority. Remember what the Bible says, "Thou shall not suffer a witch to live' (Exod. 22:18 KJV). This means that you have power over them.

CHAPTER TWENTY

SPIRITUAL DISCIPLINE

THERE ARE ATTRIBUTES which make a believer to be regarded as a disciplined Christian. A dictionary defines discipline as the treatment suited to a disciple or a learner.

The objective of discipline is to remove bad habits and to substitute good ones, such as orderliness, regularity, and obedience.

I need not add that these attributes are in line with those of a servant of God. It takes discipline to be a good servant of God. Other qualities include steadfastness and love. The Bible tells us that love is the end of the law. A disciplined believer is definitely a victorious Christian.

Follow-up

Following up fellow brethren is a very powerful attribute of a Christian. It takes discipline for a believer to follow-up a fellow Christian. This shows you care for his or her soul. It takes more than discipline; it shows love.

Visitation

Visitation is an act of love towards a brother in

Christ. Jesus said, 'I was sick and you did not visit me. I was thirsty and you gave me no water. I was naked and ye gave me no clothes.'

Prayer life

Praying for a fellow believer is also an act of discipline and love.

Study life

Spiritual discipline will move you to study. The Bible says, 'Study to show yourself approved,' a work man that needs not to be ashamed, but rightly dividing the Word of truth, (2Tim 2:15 KJV).

Holy living

'Be ye holy for I am holy,' said the Lord. Holy living is evidence of discipline in a Christian's life. An irresponsible person cannot handle spiritual things effectively, the reason being that he or she is carnal and therefore cannot please God, according to the book of Romans.

Faith

Have you ever wondered why some people find it difficult to believe in God? The answer may be that they have neither discipline nor faith in themselves, because it takes discipline to believe in God. The Bible says that he that cometh to God must believe that He is. Believe in who God says He is and keep fighting your fight of faith: 'But without faith it is impossible to please Him, for he that cometh to God must believe that He is, and that He is a rewarder of them that diligently seek Him' (Heb. 11:6 KJV).

Obedience

Obedience plays a major part in the life of a Christian or believer. God honours and rewards obedience; It takes discipline to be obedient. Jesus was obedient unto death: 'Let this mind be in you which was also in Christ Jesus. Who being in form of God, thought it not robbery to be equal with God. But made Himself of no reputation, and took upon him the form of a servant, and was made in the likeness of men: And being found in fashion as a man, he humbled himself, and became obedient unto death, even the death of the cross' (Phil. 2:5-8 KJV).

Steadfastness

In the book of Colossians Saint Paul exhorted the Christians thus: 'For though I be absent in the flesh, yet am I with you in the spirit, joying and beholding your order, and the steadfastness of your faith in Christ. As ye have therefore received Christ Jesus the Lord, so walk ye in him, rooted and built up in him and established in the faith, as ye have been taught, abounding therein with thanksgiving' (Col. 2:5 -7 KJV).

Bible Reading Is A Spiritual Weapon

Finally, fellow Christians, self -discipline should be your major attribute if you are to succeed in this race. Other measures which will help you to be steadfast in this fight will include Bible reading and meditation on the Word of God, just as God admonished Joshua: "This book of the law shall not depart out of thy mouth; but thou shalt meditate therein day and night, that thou mayest observe to do according to all that is written therein: for then thou shalt make thy way prosperous, and then thou shalt have good success' (Josh.1:8 KJV). Bible reading is also a weapon the devil cannot stand.

May I give you a testimony of what happened as I read my Bible in the middle of the night some-time ago? My family and I moved into a house that was owned by an occultist. This man was so bad, that a friend told me one day that if she had known that I was going to move into the premises, she would have discouraged me, her reason was that the owner of the house was an occultist and no one who ever lived in that house survived. Well, if I has not been a believer, I would have been scared, l:Jut I was not disturbed, neither did I regret moving in there. But the man actually attacked us in every way he knew how. He constantly attacked my husband, my children, and me spiritually. But the Lord was always with us. The attack became so frequent that one night, I was reading my Bible in the middle of the night, as my habit was, I heard some people talking by my bedroom window. 'What were they saying?' you may ask. One of them said, 'I wish she would stop reading that Bible every night.' I must tell you that I was surprised and at the same time shocked. This proofs that he had tried severally to attack me spiritually but because of my steadfastness in my Bible study, he could not succeed. What does this tell you? You can see that frequent Bible reading is a weapon of protection against the enemy, the devil, and his agents. This is why the devil will always endeavour to hinder your spiritual exercise, prayer, Bible study, and the like; if you persist, they will never succeed, and this is how your victory is achieved.

Your key to Success

God does not need any other sacrifice from us, but our righteousness through faith in the Lord Jesus Christ. For the above prayer points to be effective, you will need to be in good standing with the Lord always, and you must also be in the spirit. It follows that you will need to be sensitive in the spirit at all times, in order to know when to use these prayer bullets. The Bible encourages us to pray without ceasing, because the enemy the devil is always steadfast in his wicked acts. But the Lord admonishes us to always resist him. We can only resist him if we maintain good relationship with our Creator, whose power is supreme. We need Him (God) every minute of our lives. Go to Him through prayer for help. We need to understand that if we do not pray, there is nothing the Lord can do. When the two blind men in the book of Matthew came to Jesus to be healed of their blindness, and despite the fact that Jesus knew why they came, He still asked them, What do you want me to do for you? This encounter confirms the fact that we must take our problems to Jesus, even though He always knows what they are.

The reason is to give God the glory. Again He wants to involve us in the process; He wants to see if we recognize His supremacy. God always likes to involve His children in whatever He does, just as He involved Adam in the creation, by asking him to give names to everything He created, including Eve his helpmeet (Gen. 2:19-23).

Be Steadfast In Your Holy Fight

This is very important; do not run away from the witches nor be afraid of them, rather go close to them. Because by so doing, you will be able to weaken their evil powers and possibly save them. You can also pray for an armed robber, murderer, assassin, etc. But in doing so you must apply wisdom and be very prayerful, because there is power in the prayer of the righteous. This works wonders. I say this based on my experience.

Remember that God has not given us the spirit of fear as it is written in 2Timothy 1:7. Therefore, avoid fear, because fear torments, and fear is the weapon of the enemy, the devil. Be constant in prayer and in the study of the Word of God.

CHAPTER TWENTY-ONE

Your Mind Is the Enemy's Target

Y OU NEED TO keep your mind on check, as the enemy, the devil will always want to manipulate you through your mind; your mind therefore is a target. And whatever gets into your mind, if not dealt with, will eventually find its way into your heart; hence, the devil starts its operations in our minds. Most people do not know that almost all the problems that they encounter in their lives emanate from their mind. The Bible says that as a man thinks in his heart, so is he; hence, the enemy targets your mind. This is why you need to guard your mind, by being careful what you allow therein. Again, most of the things that take place in our lives, take place first in the spiritual realm.

Please note that you will not see the devil physically, but he acts, often times dropping ideas in your mind. The way to discern this is by comparing what he is suggesting to you with the Word of God; if it does not agree with the Word, then know that it is of the devil. What to do when you discover this is to ignore it. I strongly believe that Eve did not see the serpent physically in the Garden of Eden, neither did Jesus in the wilderness, when the devil tempted them, but all happened iff their minds. This should be a lesson to all.

Be Careful What You Expose Yourself To

Recollect that it was when Eve paid attention to the devil that the devil opened her eyes to observe that the fruit was attractive and good to be eaten: 'And when the woman saw that the tree was good for food, and that it was pleasant to the eyes, and a tree to be desired to make one wise, she took of the fruit thereof and did eat, and gave also unto her husband with her, and he did eat' (Gen 3: 6). This confirms the fact that whatever you expose yourself to, will eventually influence your life. Therefore, you should be careful in choosing the programme you watch on television or the things you listen to on the radio or the articles you read in the papers. This also applies to what you watch physically around you. Avoid those things which will impact you negatively and follow what will impact you positively. People gather, even if it is occult display; this can be dangerous.

There are several gates which let demons into our minds. These are ear, gate, eyes gate, nose gate. Therefore, be on your guard, and reject any negative thing which might filter through your mind into your heart, for in your heart are the issues of your life.

Keep Yourself Holy and Acceptable Unto God

The Bible instructs us to keep our bodies a living sacrifice. these include all our senses such as: eye, ear, nose, and mind. Again, we should be careful not to expose ourselves unduly; and more-over, we should not in any event, pay attention to the enemy's suggestions.

This is why we need to feed our hearts with the Word of God so we can meditate on them. I refer you to what the Word of God says in the book of Joshua: 'This book of the law shall not depart out of thy mouth, but thou shall meditate therein day and night, that thou mayest observe to do all that is written therein: for then thou shall make thy way prosperous, and then thou shall have good success' (Josh.1:8 KJV). This confirms the fact that whatever you meditate on affects your life, positively or negatively, depending on what it is.

We should therefore be confessing and affirming the Word of God, thinking of it and constantly reciting it in our minds. We should also act on it. If you want a quick response from God, always remind,, Him of His promises in His Word.

I thank God that we have the privilege of having the written Word of God in the form of the Bible, to teach us the ways of God.

We are more privileged than our early biblical ancestors or brethren; therefore, we are without excuse if we sin against God willingly after having known and read all their experiences and consequential outcome. If we are able to take care of our minds through prayer, by always meditating only on the Word of God and rejecting every negative thought from the enemy, we would certainly become more effective and victorious Christians.

Fear, A Weapon Of The Enemy

Fear is one of the weapons of the enemy, but if he knows that youknow your right as a child of God and can resist him, he retreats, but not far enough because he will reappear again. You may wonder why. The reason is that, he knows that he has already been cast down and doomed forever. Therefore he wants to stop you from enjoying what he is going to miss forever, Heaven.

He is forever accusing the brethren, trying to convince God why He should not bless or protect you and, why He should not admit you into His Kingdom, just as he did to Job. This is why God calls him a liar. Blessed be the God and Father of our Lord Jesus Christ who hath blessed us with all spiritual blessings in heavenly places in Christ (Eph. 1:3 KJV). Therefore, do not allow the enemy, the devil, to intimidate you with fear, lies, prayerlessness, and all his subtle tricks. For God has not given us the spirit of fear, but of power and of love and of sound mind (2Tim. 1:7 KJV).

CHAPTER TWENTY-TWO

Spiritual Warfare

L ET ME START by quoting what Wycliffe says about war and warfare: 'War is a part of the history of man as recorded in the Bible.' Spiritual warfare is therefore war between the devil and Christians. It is a very important characteristic of Christian race. Saint Paul told Timothy that he was a soldier: 'Thou therefore endure hardness as a good soldier of Jesus Christ' (2Tim. 2:3-4 NKJV). This means that every believer is a soldier for Christ. This is why we embark on warfare. He went further to say, 'No man that warreth entangleth himself with the affairs of this life; that he may please him who hath chosen him to be a soldier.' A soldier is a warrior and so every believer is a warrior. As a soldier of Jesus Christ, you need to separate yourself from the world, in order to be effective in your spiritual race.

How To Battle The Enemy

Prayer is a discipline, says Cindy Jacobs in her book Possessing the Gates of Your Enemies.

It takes discipline to develop a life of prayer. And for you to have a successful and effective prayer life, you must be disciplined and steadfast in your prayer life.

Separate Yourself

If you study the prayer life of Jesus, you will find that Jesus always separated Himself from his disciples, whenever he wanted to pray. This is very important because interference will certainly hinder your flow. In other words, there are people you associate with who may be a source of hindrance to you. You therefore will need to stay away from such people in order to stop them from pulling you down spiritually. Prayer is the only weapon which a believer has, with which to fight his spiritual battles: 'For the weapon of our warfare is not carnal but mighty through God, to the pulling down of strongholds. Casting down imaginations, and every high thing that exalteth itself against the knowledge of God, and bringing into captivity every thought to the obedience of Christ' (2Cor. 10:4-5 KJV).

Power of Praise

It is important to note that the prayer which reaches God quickly is the one associated with praise and worship. This habit should be developed if you do not already have it, and your prayer will be more interesting, because you are communicating with your heavenly Father, who enjoys the praises of His children.

Be Sensitive

A prayer warrior must be sensitive in the spirit; you must be able to receive from the Holy Spirit in order to know what to do at any given time. Remember that you are working with the Holy Spirit, who is always willing and waiting to instruct and guide you, without which you cannot succeed.

Set A Time For Yourself

It is very important to set a time for your prayer and endeavour to be there on time. Let me tell you my experience: I once planned a prayer meeting with some members of my family and other relations, and I informed them the time for the meeting. I told the Lord as well through prayer, that we would come together at a particular time. We started at the appointed time. But on one occasion, we came in about thirty minutes late; as we started to pray, I asked the Lord to descend in our midst. Guess what I heard, The

Lord immediately said to me, You came late. I have been here waiting for you. I do not need to tell you how surprised and embarrassed I was to hear what the Lord said. The God we serve is a time-conscious God. That was a big lesson to me.

Importance Of An Altar

It is very important to have an altar or a regular spot in your house for prayer. Form a habit of praying in that particular place. By so doing, you can be sure that the angels of the Lord will always be there waiting for you; and thus, the Spirit of God will flow more easily.

CHAPTER TWENTY-THREE

Put on the whole armor

I N THE BOOK of Ephesians Saint Paul listed the spiritual armor that every believer should carry ondaily basis. He told Timothy, 'You therefore must endure hardship as a good soldier of Jesus Christ' (2Tim. 2:3 KJV). Hence, as good soldiers, we should always be battle ready. Saint Paul, in the book of Ephesians, reminded us to be strong in the Lord, because we battle not against flesh and blood:

> Finally, my brethren, be strong in the Lord, (be empowered through your union with Him), and in the power of his might, (that strength which His boundless might provides). Put on the whole armor of God, that ye may be able to stand against the wiles of the devil. For we wrestle not against flesh and blood, (physical opponents), but against principalities, (master spirits), against powers, against the rulers of the darkness of this world, against spiritual wickedness in high places, (spirit forces of wickedness in the supernatural). (Eph. 6:10-18 Amp V)

Wherefore take unto you the whole armor of God (spiritual military gadgets), which include the belt of truth, breastplate of righteousness, gospel of peace, shield of faith, helmet of salvation, and the last but not the least (but very important in prayer), the sword of the spirit, which is the Word of God. Please find hereunder brief explanations of these armors:

1. Belt of truth

This means that truth helps to gird or prepare you against the attack of the enemy. Some people take pride in telling lies, without knowing that they are responsible for their misfortunes through the lies they tell.

2. Breastplate of righteousness (integrity and moral rectitude)

Have you ever bothered to ask yourself why soldiers and police men who go out to confront a mob always wear breast plate before going out to challenge them?

3. Shod your feet with the gospel of peace

Gospel is the message salvation, the good news. Please refer to page 82, the story of a sister who failed to evangelize as she was meant to do.

4. Shield of faith

A shield is, a broad piece of armor made of rigid material and strapped to the arm or carried in the hand for protection against hurled or thrust weapons. As can

Put on the whole armor

be seen, faith represents a shield, which is one of the armors used for protection against enemy's attack

5. Helmet of salvation

A helmet is a common protective head gear, such as the ones worn by motorcyclists and even cyclists. This is exactly what salvation does for us; it is meant to protect our head from a spiritual fall.

6. Sword of the spirit (the Word of God)

The sword of the spirit, which is the Word of God, is a weapon against the enemy. Therefore, the more you read it, confess it, and act it, the more victorious you will become.

7. Prayer

Needless to say, prayer 1s a weapon; a core weapon which a Christian needs to possess against the enemy. Therefore, instead of worrying and complaining, pray to God, your creator. It is to Him alone that you should complain and ask for assistance and vindication. He is your heavenly Father and is always waiting for you to bring your problems to Him for solution.

Satan's Weapons

Satan, the devil, has some weapons which he uses to attack the children of God. These weapons are fear, torment, lies, disease, anger, hatred, unconfessed sins, unforgiveness, jealousy, strife or quarrelsomeness, prayerlessness, bitterness, envy and all forms of sin. therefore, you must avoid these evils.

The Bible says we should not allow the sun to go down on our wrath. The only way to be able to resist him effectively is to let the Word of God dwell in you richly. The devil enjoys attention; therefore, do not give it to him. This follows therefore that you have to be sensitive in the spirit in order to be able to discern when he is around you. It is only through prayer and the Word of God that you can put him to flight. Constantly believe, confess, and put the Word of God into action. Please refer to the section on prayer bullets.

Resist the Devil

The devil is always looking for loopholes through which it can afflict the children of God; therefore, you must resist him by all means and at all cost. The Bible has admonished us to resist the devil, Submit yourselves therefore to God. Resist the devil, and he will flee from you' (James 4:7 KJV). You cannot do without God. In other words, you cannot do it carnally or by your own power. Jesus says, 'Without me ye can do nothing, I am the vine, ye are the branches: He that abideth [hooked] in me, and I in him, the same bringeth forth much fruit: for without me ye can do nothing (John 15:5 KJV). The fruit you bear depends on how much of the Word of God you have inside you. For you to be victorious over the devil therefore, you must live your life according to the doctrine of Christ.

Abundant Life

Jesus came to give us abundant life, and this includes victory over the enemy in the areas such as sickness, financial well-being, peace of mind that passes all understanding, and total well being. Jesus says, 'The thief cometh not but for to steal, and to kill, and to destroy. I am come that they might have life, and that they might have it more abundantly (John 10:10 KJV).

The Devil is a Deceiver

The devil is always out to deceive you, making you feel or say things like 'God knows my needs, so I do not need to pray.' This is the reason why you should not procrastinate in your prayer life.

Knowing this, therefore, when you feel lazy to pray, beware that it is the manipulation of the devil. He does this because he knows that when you pray, God will answer. Secondly, he will not be able to afflict you with his evil plans, because God will show you a way out of your problems. Thirdly, he will not let you pray because when you do, his kingdom will suffer a quake and, dislocation in the form of confusion, frustration and incoherence.

The devil has the tendency to be very subtle; he will bite you but also blow on you, and make you feel he is on your side.

He hits you and watches your   reaction. As soon

as he observes that you are fearful, he starts suggesting things that will lure you into committing sin against God. This way he can accuse you before the Lord. He does this in order to afflict you the more, just as he did to Job, also Eve in the Garden of Eden. But because Job was very steadfast with the Lord, the enemy could not prevail over him; rather, God blessed Job the more, so much that, at the end of Job's temptations, Job had more than he had before the temptation. The Bible says that Job was upright: "There was a man in the land of Uz whose name was Job; and that man was perfect and upright, and one that feared God and eschewed evil" (Job 1:1). I encourage you to read the book of Job, and see how the devil tried to destroy him, and to pull him down from his faith in his God. Because Job was a God-fearing man, the devil failed in his attempt with Job. This is the type of relationship every Christian should have with God.

If there is anything that the devil is afraid of, it is prayer. Each time a believer prepares to pray, the devil will always put up a fight. It usually comes through procrastination, laziness, postponement, unnecessary interruptions, sleepy eyes, slumber, tiredness, and the like. Having known this, you will need to watch out for such symptoms and prepare to resist him. The Bible says resist the devil and he will flee. All that the devil needs is a little resistance, because he is a coward, and will flee.

It is of utmost importance that you remain in the spirit, in order to be able to discern his tactics.

Put on the whole armor

Some of the Devil's Tricks

Some people are so lazy to pray, so much that when they are asked to pray, they will say, 'Oh, don't worry, God knows my problems.' This is a lie of the enemy, the devil. Yes, God knows your problems, but He still wants you to bring those problems to him, because He will never do anything you have not asked Him to do. The reason being probably because He wants to know if you have faith in Him. Again, He will not want you to blame Him like Adam did in the Garden of Eden. When Adam disobeyed God in the garden by eating the forbidden fruit, he blamed it on his wife, Eve. He answered God by saying, It is the woman you gave me, who made me to eat it. Indirectly, he was blaming God.

Furthermore, God wants to see if you recognise His supremacy or believe in what He says He can do. There are instances in the Bible of people who came to Jesus for healing, for instance, the two blind men, and Jesus asked them, What do you want me to do for you? It does not mean that Jesus did not know what their problem was, but He wanted to involve them in the process of solving their problems. So, dear friend, always go to God in humility and tell Him about your problems instead of complaining.

CHAPTER TWENTY-FOUR

The Drama in the Garden of Eden

L ET US NOW take a look at what happened in the Garden of Eden between God, Adam, Eve and the Serpent.

> Then the Lord God took the man and put him in the Garden of Eden to tend and keep it. And the Lord God commanded the man, saying, 'Of every tree of the garden you may freely eat; but of the tree of the knowledge of good and evil you shall not eat, for in the day that you eat of it you shall surely die.' (Gen. 2:15-16 NKJV)

The Bible describes the serpent as being more cunning than any beast:

> Now the serpent was more cunning than any beast of the field which the Lord God made. And he said to the woman, Has God indeed said, "'You shall not eat of every tree of the garden?'"
>
> And the woman said to the serpent, We may eat the fruit of the tree of the garden; but

of the fruit of the tree which is in the midst of the garden, God has said, "You shall not eat it, nor shall you touch it, lest you die."' The serpent said to the woman, You will not surely die. For God knows that in the day you eat of it your eyes will be opened, and you will be like God, knowing good and evil.

So when the woman saw that the tree was good for food, that it was pleasant to the eyes, and a tree desirable to make one wise, she took of its fruit and ate. She also gave to her husband with her, and he ate. (Gen. 3:1-6 NKJV).

Eve instantly believed the serpent. Oh, what a shame. Not only did she eat it, she gave it to her husband! And he ate. This is the man to whom the Lord handed down a command not to eat of the fruit. First of all, the woman sinned by believing the serpent instead of going to her husband to ask for clearance. Again, Eve should have sought her husband's consent prior to attempting to eat the fruit, but she decided to experiment it alone. Regrettably, Adam did not put his foot down as one to whom the command was personally handed down. As a result, both sinned and fell from grace. I am convinced that if Eve had really known God and His Word, she would have resisted the serpent more sternly. She did not resist the clevil, rather she gave in to the devil's first attempt. Question for your thought: Why did the serpent not go to the man, instead went to the woman? The answer is 'Because he always targets the women, knowing that they are the weaker sex.' Women should always be vigilant. His tactics have not changed; he is always attacking the families and, in most cases, through the woman.

The Blame Game

Let us briefly examine the consequences of their sin and subsequent fall:

I.   Their eyes opened.
II. They saw their nakedness.
III. They hid from God.
IV. The man blamed the woman.
V.   The woman blamed the serpent.
VI. And then came the curse upon mankind.

Allow me to say that it was because the woman paid attention to the devil, hence she observed that the fruit was attractive, and then the urge to eat it arose in her. We must therefore be careful what we pay attention to, because the devil is very subtle in his ways.

Create No Loophole For The Devil

The devil is always looking for a loophole through which he can afflict the children of God; therefore, you must do your best to resist him at all cost. He operates through such tricks as anger, hatred, unconfessed sins, lack of forgiveness, jealousy, strife, disagreement, prayerless life, bitterness, envy, and the like. Therefore, be wise and do not fall prey to such temptations.

Let me elaborate on some of the devil's tricks listed above:

Strife: Strife is the act of contending for superiority through earnest endeavour, violent contention, fight, bitter conflict, heated (often violent) dissension resulting from absence of agreement.

Bitterness: Bitterness is the state of being bitter, sharp, or acrid in either a literal or figurative sense; it is implacableness (incapable of being pacified), resentfulness, vexation of mind.

Envy: Envy means malice, ill will, spite, uneasiness at the sight of another's excellence or good fortune.

Unforgiveness: The Bible says, 'Let not the sun go down on your wrath.' The only way to be able to resist him effectively is to let the Word of God dwell richly in you. The devil enjoys attention; therefore, ignore him. In order to be able to defeat him, you should continually confess, believe, and act out (put into action) the Word of God. Please note that some of the statements are repeated at various points in order to buttress the concept _ due to its importance.

Your Prayer Life

Engage yourself in fervent (sincere and intense) and effectual prayer. Effectual means effective, constructive, and productive prayer. For effective prayer language, please see the section on prayer bullets, to remind yourself of the right language to use in your prayer. This language will surely put the devil and his agents to flight.

Wisdom For Victory

Again I will like to advise you not to avoid witches, armed robbers, murderers, assassins, such like, should you know them. You can lead them to Christ; it will surprise you to see that you can prevail against their evil attacks, and will make them hold you in awe.

If you pray for them, their power will be weakened, and eventually they could repent and be saved. This really works, and I speak from experience, because there is power in the prayer of the righteous, according to the book of James. Find a way of getting close to them so that you can minister to them because by so doing, you will be able to reduce their powers and their ability to carry out evil activities. Besides you may also be able to deliver them from being used by the enemy.

CHAPTER TWENTY-FIVE

Jesus' Prayer Life

I HAVE ALWAYS wondered at how much time Jesus assigned to prayer. It should challenge. anyone who calls himself or herself a child of God. Jesus' prayer life is worthy of emulation. You cannot succeed without commitment to prayer. Jesus' lifestyle was predominantly one of prayer. He regarded prayer more than anything else; in other words, He made prayer a priority in His life. After His baptism, He was led up to the mountain fasting, and of course you know that fasting goes with prayer; In other words, fasting and prayer are interchangeable. To put it in another way, fasting induces prayer. Jesus was very good at both. This was why He was able to defeat the devil when He was tempted on the mountain,

When He had been baptized, Jesus came up immediately from the water; and behold, the heavens were opened to Him, and He saw the Spirit of God descending like a dove and alighting upon Him ... And Jesus was led by the Spirit into the wilderness to be tempted by the devil. And when He had fasted forty days and forty nights, afterward He was hungry. Now when the tempter came to Him, he said, "If you are the Son of God ...." command that these stones become bread. But He answered and said, It is written, Man shall not live by bread alone, but by every word that proceeds from the mouth of God. (Matt. 3:16; 4:1 -11 NKJV)

The devil did not stop there, but continued to suggest things to Jesus But the Lord Jesus countered him, 'It is written. Of course the devil was defeated because he has no power over the Word of God, as the Word of God is powerful. The point to note here is that it was prayer that gave the Lord Jesus Christ victory over the enemy. Note also that at the end of the temptation, the enemy left Him, and immediately angels came and ministered to Him. This proves that God is always watching our everyday life and is ever ready to celebrate us when we defeat the enemy.

My House Shall Be Called The House Of Prayer

Jesus told those gamblers who were using the temple of God as trading and gambling point, 'My house shall be called the house of prayer.'

And when He had come into Jerusalem, all the city was moved, saying, Who is this? So the multitude said, 'This is Jesus, the prophet from Nazareth of Galilee. Then Jesus went into the temple of God and drove out all those who bought and sold in the temple, and overturned the tables of the money changers and the seats of those who sold doves. And He said to them, It is written, "My house shall be called a house of prayer, but you have made it into a den of thieves.' (Matt. 21:10-13, Luke 19:46 NKJV)

As you can see from the above, Jesus had a great passion for prayer and would never permit anything contrary to prayer to be done in the house of God, His Father. Those ministers who turn the house of God into a trading ground for things like anointing oil, handkerchiefs and so on should take note.

This Type Goeth Not But By Prayer And Fasting

Some of the afflictions we suffer can easily be taken care of by fasting and prayer. The Bible is our standard. Find here what the Lord Jesus Christ told His disciples when they were unable to cast out the demon from a person possessed by a deaf and dumb spirit.

And when He came to the disciples, He saw a great multitude around them, and scribes disputing with them. Immediately, when they saw Him, all the people were greatly amazed, and running to Him, greeted Him. And He asked the scribes, What are you discussing with them? Then one of the crowd answered and said, Teacher, I brought You my son, who has a mute spirit. And wherever it seizes him, it throws him down; he foams at the mouth, gnashes his teeth, and becomes rigid. So I spoke to your disciples, that they should cast it out, but they could not.' He answered him and said, 'O faithless generation, how long shall I be with you? How long shall I bear with you? Bring him to Me.' Then they brought him to Him. And when He saw him, immediately the spirit convulsed him, and he fell on the ground and wallowed, foaming at the mouth.

Observe above that demons know who you are. Please read for yourself all that transpired in this passage for better understanding.

When Jesus saw that the people came running together, He rebuked the unclean spirit, saying to it: 'Deaf and dumb spirit, I command you, come out of him and   enter him no more!' (Mark 9:14 -19, 9:25 NKJV)

Note that Jesus called the unclean spirit by· name. He did not just say, 'Come out.' Secondly, apart from prayer and fasting,Jesus cited faithlessness as one of the things which hindered His disciples from casting out the deaf and dumb spirit. Without gainsaying, faith plays a major part in our prayer life.

Men Ought Always To Pray

Hear what Jesus told His disciples about prayer. Before then, He made reference to what happened during the time of Noah and Lot, how people were marrying and giving to marriage, drank, ate, and so on, until the day Noah entered the ark. And the flood came and destroyed them all because they were living in sin. And in the case of Lot, so it happened until the day Lot went out of Sodom it rained fire and brimstone from heaven and destroyed them all.

Then He said men ought always to pray (probably because we do not know when it will happen in our own lives' time). Well, my take is this, even if Jesus tarries till two hundred years to come, what is man's lifespan? I think we should live our lives as though Jesus is coming the next minute. Let the sinner beware.

And He went further to advise them, saying that men should always pray and not give up. And told them the parable of a judge that feared not God nor respected man. The judge was so bad that he even admitted that he neither feared God nor respected man.

There was in a city a judge, who did not fear God nor regarded man. Now there was a widow in that city; and she came to him saying, 'Get justice for me from my adversary.' And he would not for a while; but afterward he said within himself, 'Though I do not fear God nor regard man, yet because this widow troubles me I will avenge her lest by her continual coming she weary me.' And the Lord Jesus said, hear what the unjust judge said. And shall not God avenge His own elect, [His chosen ones] which cry day and night unto Him though he bear long with them? I tell you he will avenge them speedily, nevertheless when the Son of man cometh, shall he find faith on the earth? (Luke 18:1-8 NKJV)

May I explain here that the elect is the person, who is yet to be saved? Jesus is saying here that though the Lord is waiting for them to come to Him, through faith in Christ's atonement death on the cross, God will still answer their prayers if they call upon His name persistently. In anotp.er version, He calls it importunity. This means that the elects have a part to play in their salvation'. through prayer. If God will answer an unsaved person who calls upon Him, how much more will he answer the prayer of the redeemed child of His? What are you waiting for?

Separate Yourself

Jesus took prayer seriously. He always separated Himself for prayers. Even after the miracle of five loaves and two fishes, Jesus left his disciples and went away to pray alone. Now let us see what happened after that prayer: *And when he had sent them away, he departed into a mountain to pray. And when even was come, the ship was in the midst of the sea and He was. alone on the land. And He saw them toiling in rowing; for the wind was contrary unto them, and about the fourth watch of the night He cometh unto them, walking upon the sea, and would have passed by them.* The main reason is that this is the only means by which He could communicate with His Father. Again prayer is the only source of spiritual strength. Note that it was after this prayer that His disciples saw him walking on the sea.] *But when they saw him walking upon the sea, they supposed it had been a spirit, and they cried out'* (Mark 6:46-49 NKJV). If you read further, you will find that it was on this occasion that Jesus invited Peter when Peter found out that it was Jesus, and he asked Jesus to bid him come, and Jesus bid him come. But along the way his faith waned and he began to sink. It goes to show that Godwill strengthen you if you constantly fellowship with Him when you mix it with faith. Hence, God likes us to come to Him, so that He would endow us with His power for exploits, that we may be able to tread on serpents and on scorpions, as promised in the book of Luke 10: 19.

CHAPTER TWENTY-SIX

Overcoming Temptation

JESUS ADMONISHED HIS disciples to pray lest they fell into temptation. In other words, a believer who does not pray can easily fall into temptation. This is true. Before His crucifixion, Jesus told his disciples how exceedingly sorrowful, even to the point of death, he was.

He told them to stay and watch with him that night. But his disciples could not keep up with him. When he came back, he found them sleeping; hence, He rebuked them: 'Then cometh Jesus with them unto a place called Gethsemane and said unto the disciples, Sit ye here while I go and pray yonder. He took with Him Peter and two sons of Zebedee, and began to be sorrowful and very distressed. "Watch and pray lest you enter into temptation," He told them' (Matt. 26:37-41 NKJV).

Do you know that Jesus prayed three times that night before he was taken away for crucifixion signifying it was the will of God for Him to have been crucified? Not praying can lead you into temptation. Beware, because the enemy the devil is watching, looking for an opportunity through which he may devour you. The Bible says that devil goes about, seeking who to devour, like a roaring lion.

Jesus Promoted Some Of His Disciples To Apostles

The Lord Jesus Christ prayed all night before He chose His disciples: Now it came to pass in those days that He went out to the mountain to pray, and continued all night in prayer to God. And when it was day, He called His disciples to Himself; and from them He chose twelve whom He also named apostles; And He came down with them and stood on a level place with a crowd of His disciples and a great multitude of people from all Judea and Jerusalem and from the seacoast of 'lyre and Si'don, who came to hear Him and he healed them of their diseases (Luke 6:12 -17 NKJV). The lesson here is that Jesus never did anything without praying. The big question is, Why did Jesus choose Judas Iscariot, the man who betrayed Him along with them, even after having prayed all night? The answer is very simple. The Word of God must be fulfilled. Therefore after you must prayed, allow the will of God to be done, even as Jesus prayed in the Garden of Gethsemane.

Dismantling Of Satan's Crusade Ground

Let me pause here and give a testimony of what happened in Port Harcourt, Rivers State of Nigeria, which happens to be my State of origin. The city of Port Harcourt is the capital of Rivers State in Nigeria. As Christianity continued to take its root in the state, the enemy, the devil, intensified his grip upon the land, but thank God, who never looses a battle. What I am about to narrate took place in the late 1980s. After a flyover was built in the area popularly known as Isaac Boro Park, the area around the bridge lying waste and underutilized, and consequently became a gambling spot and hideout for hoodlums, and all sorts of miscreants. The area turned into a trading venue for all sorts of artifacts and satanic images for magicians and idol worshipers.

Before long, these abominable acts spread in the area like wildfire, and the place became a terrible sight. This area is on a major road leading to the State's Secretariat Complex, through which workers go to work from every part of the State, and therefore, is a very busy spot because it was and still is a connecting point from every part of the state.

This secretariat accommodates many ministries and office blocks for the workers. I was still working then; therefore, it was my regular route. One day as I was returning from work, I became very angry in the spirit and decided to do something, as I was moved by the Spirit of God. Then I started stretching my hand at any spot wherever I saw them displaying, to cancel the activities of the Satanic agents. This I continued to do wherever I saw such display. After about two weeks to my surprise, this display gradually began to disappear. When I saw this, I was encouraged to continue; eventually, the entire area was spiritually sanitized and became a clean and orderly place. Not long after the Government of the State turned the place into an interstate motor park, and a big shopping centre. God can use our prayer to change things. Do not wait for someone else to do it; God is waiting for you.

When Ye Pray, Believe

After Jesus cursed the fig tree, His disciples were surprised that the simple words He spoke to the fig tree immediately manifested; Jesus merely said "Let no fruit grow on you." When His disciples wondered, Jesus told them, 'Have faith in God. For verily I say unto you that whosoever shall say unto this mountain, Be thou removed, and be thou cast into the sea; and shall not doubt in his heart, but shall believe that those things which he saith shall come to pass, he shall have whatsoever he saith. Therefore I say unto you, what things soever ye desire, when ye pray, believe that ye receive them, and ye shall have them' (Mark 11:2-24 KJV). Recall that the Lord Jesus Christ said that faith is as small as a mustard seed.

CHAPTER TWENTY-SEVEN

Help From Above

I WISH TO start by quoting what the Bible says about how the Holy Spirit helps in our prayer: 'Likewise the Spirit also helps in our weaknesses. For we do not know what we should pray for as we ought, but the Spirit Himself makes intercession for us with groanings which cannot be uttered' (Romans 8:26 NKJV). This means that the Holy Spirit helps us in our prayer when we do not know what to pray about; therefore, when we are in such situations, we should always endeavour to yield to the Holy Spirit's directive instead of giving up. This can only be done if you know the Word of God, and are also alert in the spirit. For instance, I may want to pray for my ministry, but do not know exactly the area to channel my prayer. At this point the Holy Spirit steps in to help if you yield. For the Holy Spirit to help you, you should have accepted the Lord Jesus as your personal Lord and Saviour. Even after this, you will still need to ask God for the Holy Spirit before He can help you, please see Luke 11:9-13, this is very important. A renowned man of God had this to say: You may know what to pray, but may not know how to pray. When we pray in the spirit, there is an amplification of our victory

(Pastor Adrian Rogers, of blessed memory). The Holy Spirit, because He is a spirit, knows what is happening in the spiritual, because everything good or bad emanates in the spiritual. The desire to pray may be inborn and may become obvious at a certain stage in one's life. It is then that you will begin to have a strong desire to pray, as you begin to go through some difficult situations in your life. God allows this and wants to train you and bring out what He had already deposited in you. You do not have to be a prayer warrior in order to pray. Every obstacle you go through in your life will only be solved through prayer; therefore, pray without ceasing.

Power in the Blood

I heard some men of God condemn the sprinkling of the blood of Jesus. They say that there is nowhere in the Bible where the blood of Jesus was sprinkled. But they forget that in the book of Revelation, we are told that we overcame the devil with word of our testimonies and the blood of the lamb. To counter such men of God, let me narrate this testimony of what the Holy Spirit told me some time ago while I was on my knees, praying. As I prayed one night and it happened to be at midnight, I heard a terrifying stampede by a religious sect in white garment. They sang and marched down the street, the entire atmosphere was charged and thrown into chaos and fear. While on my knees,, I was hearing dogs in the neighbourhood barking loudly and fiercely; while the sound of the stampede was such as to make me wonder what was happening. There and then I was almost griped with fear. It was at that point that the Lord said to me, 'Saturate, Saturate.' Whereupon I asked, 'Saturate what?' And the Lord said, 'Saturate the blood of Jesus into the atmosphere.' Then I started sprinkling the blood of Jesus into the entire atmosphere. Immediately I saturated the blood of Jesus into the atmosphere, the dogs stopped barking, and there was confusion in the midst of the evil sect. The Lord thus gave us victory that night, and if I may add, there was a political struggle in the land at that time, and the leader of that sect was vying for a very high office in the state; The importance of the power in the blood of Jesus can never be overemphasised. One of the reasons why God shed the blood of His Son was to help us defeat the enemy the devil, (refer to Revelation 12:11). You should spread the blood of Jesus at him once you are born again.

The Devil Will Fight You When You Give Your Life To Christ, But The Holy Spirit Will Help You

After my husband gave his life to Christ, the devil tried very vehemently to take his life, so much that I began to hear gunshots in the spiritual within our residence. I say spiritual, because whenever I heard the gunshots, I would go out to check, but to my surprise, I would see no one. One day, when I was with my husband in the room, I heard these gunshots again, but to my surprise, when I asked my husband, he said he did not hear it.

When the devil could not take his (my husband's) life, he tried another strategy. This time around, he got my husband so sick that his lips became very reddish and sore, but he still managed to go to work. The next day as my husband was returning from work and as he alighted from his car walking towards the house, I observed that he was staggering. As I wondered at him, the devil whispered to me thus: 'See your husband, he has caught AIDS, [a severe immunological disorder caused by the retrovirus HIV, the human immunodeficiency virus]. See how his lips are red.' I kept my eyes on him for two days and refused to say anything because I was engrossed in anger. On the third day, it struck me that the devil was trying to get me to react negatively. I resisted him, as the Spirit of the Lord moved me, and I said, 'Devil you are a liar. You don't want me to kiss my husband.' And I immediately, defied the devil and went to kiss my husband. Believe it or not, after that kiss, my husband got healed of the redness of the lips, without having to take any medication. I make haste to tell you that my husband has a lovely kissing lips, and the devil was only being jealous, but God gave me victory over him, because I listened to the voice of the Holy Spirit.

It pays to be in the spirit. If not for the Holy Spirit, I would have accused my husband of infidelity, and the consequences to our marriage would have been catastrophic.

The Devil's Second Strategy

You would not believe that the devil did not stop there; he tried another ploy and. this time around, he afflicted my husband with serious sickness which kept him in bed for two days.

As I went into the room to check his condition, he whispered to me that he was very weak, and this happened late into the night. Before this time, I had an encounter with the Lord during the day; I had a visitation by the Lord. His hand was upon me, so that I was feeling fire all over me. My head was so hot that I began to scream, and my husband's niece whose name is Juliet, watched me while gripped in fear. She then called out 'Sisi' as she usually calls me and asked, 'What is the matter?' And I replied in a loud voice screaming: 'It is Jesus.' It was so much that I had to tell her to lay hand upon my head, to reduce the heat. By the way, she was a born-again Christian. As she laid her hands upon my head, and prayed for me, the heat subsided, while she contacted the fire herself. Today the Lord is using her. As I was saying, when my husband whispered to me that he was very weak, I was afraid, and thought of going out that night to invite a nearby brother who happened to live about a mile away, to come and pray for him, because there was no phone. The time was 1:am in the morning. I thought to myself, how can I call out someone at this time of the night and immediately, the Holy Spirit spoke to me and said, '**Go and pray**

for him, this was why I anointed you earlier in the evening.' I am glad to say that my husband received his healing after I prayed for him instantly and was able to go to work that morning. Praise the Lord. Prayer works wonders, when the Holy Spirit leads you.

There are other numerous testimonies of what the Lord has done for me through prayer which I am unable to narrate here but rest assured that God answers prayers.

CHAPTER TWENTY-EIGHT

Personal Testimonies

Miraculous provision of a house

T HE LORD WROUGHT a great miracle in my family some years ago ranging from salvation to blessings. He proved to me that He rewards His children (the saved Christians) according to their faith in Him.

Most of the problems we face is as a result of our ignorance. Myself and my husband gave our lives to Christ a year after one another. My husband suddenly lost his job, after which something miraculous happened. One day, my husband returned from his work place to tell me that it was over, I asked him, what was over? Since there was no prior indication or sign that he had a problem. On further enquiry, he told me, still in a state of shock, that he did not know why and that he did nothing wrong. He went further to say that he was made to sign 1,000, official letters which of course was a part of his job schedule as a Chief Personnel Officer of the organization. My husband is a hardworking man who would not seek gratification for any good done; hence, he was liked by many in the corporation. The humiliation was that he was made to sign the letters shortly after they made the decision to terminate his appointment. This decision was wickedness of the highest order.

After he told me the ugly incident, I felt really downcast, but God strengthened me. I would like to say here that three weeks before the episode, I had a dream which revealed to me that my husband was in trouble, and in that dream he appeared helpless as he walked towards me and the jacket he was wearing fell off him, but the Lord spoke to me these words in that dream as I watched him looking distressed: 'Thou shall be strong, thou shall be saved, no evil shall befall you.' I remembered it word for word because I woke up and wrote it down. I must tell you that I did not know what was going to happen, until my husband lost his job, whereupon the Holy Ghost reminded me of that dream.

Shortly after my husband lost his job the battle for our official residence started. After my husband lost his job, I had another dream, where I saw our official residence floating on top of water; it was dreadful, and I enquired of the Lord what to do. The Lord told me to fast for three days, which I did. It was not long after, that the battle for the house started; culminating into notice to vacate the property. When this happened, I became angrier in my spirit, but I held onto God; my thought was, my husband did not deserve what happened to him. Before we knew it, this property was earmarked for sale, because someone in the Corporation was interested in buying it. So keen was the person that she engaged a very high-ranking military officer to help her secure the property.

I knew this fact because the Officer who come frequently to threaten us to vacate the property told me that an Army General was interested in the property. I was amused in my spirit and told the Housing Officer that I had many Generals with me as I stood with him. I was sure that he did not understand what I meant. I say this because as children of God, we have unseen angels guarding and guiding us. Again, the Lord says that His children should be as bold as a lion, and that whatever we say in faith, we shall receive same.

We took a decision to apply to buy the house since we were living there, Prior to our application, the person who wanted to throw us out and possess the house, had met the Governor, but because we were occupying the house, the Governor did not know what to do. He decided to give us impossible and conflicting conditions. He also gave us a very short notice within which to pay for the house; and also asked us to pay in full; which does not apply when one is buying a government property. The aim was to deny or prevent us from buying the property.

God's intervention: One night, the Lord woke me up to pray, and when I looked at the time, it was about 1:00 a.m. Without any clue as to what to pray about, I started blasting in tongues, with my voice piercing through the midst of the night. Remember that when you are in a certain state of mind and you are praying, your mood is always mixed with emotion as well as anger in the spirit and more so when your eyes are heavy with sleep. My husband had travelled to the village, hence I felt free; I mean I did not have any fear of interruption. When I finished praying, and as I was about to lie down to sleep, the Lord commanded me, 'Go and read your Bible.' My eyes were so heavy with sleep, coupled with the fact that I had no clue where to read, I only flipped open the Bible and started reading, not taking note of where or what portion of the Bible that I was reading, as I wanted to go back to bed, a voice started echoing in the room, and I heard: 'The Lord is a man of war, and the Lord is His name.' Then I started looking around, wondering where the voice was coming from or who was speaking. Suddenly it occurred to me to check if that was in the portion I read. You would not believe that it was exactly the portion I read; and it was in (Exodus 15:3). I was stunned at how the Word popped out of the Bible and was speaking to me. This goes to prove that the Word of God is a living Word. Something happened after this prayer; and you could never have guessed it. Two days after this prayer, we received a letter from the Government, to purchase the property. This was exactly why the Lord woke me up to pray. This again goes to prove that midnight prayer is very powerful.

After the loss of my husband's job, I was to travel to Benin City in Nigeria for a women's Christian convention, known as Christian Women Fellowship International (CWFI), but I could not make up my mind whether or not to attend. My fear was, what if by the time I came back, my family had been evicted from the house? Suddenly, a voice asked me, "Are you the one that had been protecting them?" I realised it was the Lord speaking to me, and thereupon, I made up my mind to attend the convention. On the last day, just as we were about to depart for home, the host, Archbishop Benson Idahosa of blessed memory, said to all of us "Go, there is a miracle awaiting you." Without hesitation, I claimed it'

Surprisingly, soon after I had returned, the Spirit of God moved me to do things that surprised everyone, including myself. I started decorating the premises with coloured bulbs and so on. It was at this juncture that the battle started, and the Lord took over.

Again, the Lord gave me boldness to resist them; I did it of course through prayer. At this stage, my husband had not been paid any money, not even gratuity, having been terminated without notice. This made my anger more intense. But I challenged God and reminded Him that we had always worshipped Him day and night in that house and that I knew He had prepared someone, to give us the needed money with which to pay for the property. I prayed to the Lord to direct the person's footsteps toward us, and that was exactly what the Lord did.

I prayed to God to intervene on our behalf, and after praying, I believed that the Lord had answered my prayer, and thereafter I did not exercise fear anymore. I was therefore not surprised, when on return from work, my husband told me that someone came offering to rent the property, and that on seeing the house, he remarked that even though he required a house, the one in question was bigger than what he was looking for. Furthermore, my husband told me that the man said that he believed that God wanted to perform a miracle, and that he would like to be a part of it. Being a brother in the Lord, my husband told him everything about the house. My husband informed me that the man invited him to come to his office the next day and collect the money with which to pay for the property. At this time we had advertised the property in order to raise the money with which to buy the property. My husband hardly could believe the man. Therefore, when he told me, I told him to go and that God was at work. The next day my husband went to the man, and the man gave him a cheque, to cover the exact amount we needed to pay for the property, without asking for collateral, witness, or surety. And he never bordered us. But it was after sometime had passed, say about two months after we had rented the house, without anyone informing him, the man became anxious for his money. It became clear that the man acted under the influence of the Holy Spirit, and that God was in control all along. May God be praised, for He is a faithful God, no one can deny it.

I must not forget to mention another thing the Lord revealed with reference to the above miracle: as soon as we paid for the house, that very moment, the young man who was coming to the compound to intimidate me with the fact that an army General was involved concerning the house, appeared, and I told him that we had paid for the house; the man burst into tears. This confirmed the fact that the governor must have threatened them to make sure we did not buy the house, again the Lord proved Himself to be Supreme. Hallelujah.

Shrines Destroyed

God has used my ministry to pull down many strongholds of the enemy, including shrines, which I will not mention here, for some obvious reasons. For instance there were areas which people used to dread which have now become express roads and housing estates in Port Harcourt; similarly in other places and communities.

Victory in Wizard's Coven

1. God took us to a house belonging to an occultist where they carried out witchcraft practices; In the place, we experienced all types of spiritual attacks. I think God was training me to be bold in my prayers and not fear. The attacks were so severe that the occultist, was very anxious for us to move out because of our fervent prayers and God's intervention. As a result of our prayers, his evil operations were being frustrated. One day, he attempted to attack me physically within the compound. On this fateful day, I went out, and on returning and about to enter the compound, I observed

the man pacing up and down in anger, around the gate. As he saw me, he behaved as though he was coming towards me. I was cautious, and later prayed in my spirit, as I was almost gripped with fear. After a while, the Lord emboldened me, and I moved towards him, and asked, Is anything wrong? He was startled, and it was as though he suddenly regained consciousness, and he answered, 'No, no, nothing.' I then walked past him and went straight to my flat. Who says prayer does not work? God preserved me and my family and led us out of that place intact to His own glory. Did He not promise us in His Word? "Behold I give unto you power to tread on serpents and scorpions, and over all the power of the enemy, and nothing shall by any means hurt you' (Luke 10:19 KJV).

2. *Witches' coven*: The Lord took me again to a building where witches used to have their meetings, this time in a country, in Europe; this was another training ground. Again, the Lord gave me victory, through various prayer terms and heavenly languages (tongues). He even converted some of them to His own glory.

3. *An occultist handed himself over to the Lord*: In my former workplace, a man who usually attacked me because of my prayers suddenly bought himself a Bible, when he could not prevail against me. In the end, he surrendered himself to the Lord in a nearby Church and came to my office in excitement to tell me he had converted to Christianity.

Fish Bone In The Throat, Broken By God

My daughter had a fish bone that hung across her throat, and every attempt to bring it out proved abortive. I then took her to a doctor who, after examination informed me that the only option was to have an operation. I rejected it, took my daughter home and prayed, telling God to do it by himself, and went to sleep. The next morning, my daughter, who was about four years old then, called me, saying, 'Mummy, come and see.' When I went to look: I was amazed at what I saw, the Lord had broken the bone which was as big as an office pin into pieces. The Lord had dipped His hand into her throat and got the bones broken without an operation, and she did not feel any pain during and after. Is God not good?

Lead (Lode) In My Chest Miraculously Disappeared

I once had a funny feeling inside me; it felt like I had a metal moving inside my chest; it was excruciatingly painful; I mean it felt like my chest was going numb. It was like a broken nib or pencil tip, and I was feeling a sharp movement inside my chest. I felt as if my entire chest was becoming lifeless. I wondered what could be happening to me. It was as though it was moving towards my heart. Suddenly, I decided to pray, and immediately after I had prayed, the pain miraculously disappeared. I could not believe it; it was as though I was delivered from a violent attack. If that thing had got to my heart, I would definitely have died. But God immediately took control. I thank God for answering my prayers and keeping me alive.

Urine Diverted From A Wrong Tract

The devil is out to try the believers in various ways through subtle means. One day, I felt my urine deliberately refusing to flow through its normal track, but rather appeared as though it was going to come out through my mouth. I got angry in the spirit and commanded the urine to follow its natural course, and it instantly obeyed. The above two experiences show how the devil deliberately tries to inflict us with illnesses and diseases. If I were not in the spirit and applying my powers in the Word of God, and pleading the blood of Jesus, it would have landed me in the hospital, and I probably would have died. There is no medical remedy to spiritual problems except prayer. Thank God for Jesus and the Holy Spirit. I have had to write down the above testimonies for the benefit of other believers whom the devil may be tormenting now or may do so in the future. Do not panic, just believe that there is power in the blood of Jesus and exercise your faith.

CHAPTER TWENTY-NINE

Testimonies in the Ministry

A S HAD EARLIER been stated in previous chapters, the Lord has wrought many miracles in this ministry. Please read below.

Seven Years Broken Marriage Healed

A woman who had moved out of her matrimonial home for seven years, as a result of a breakdown of the marriage came to me crying. In the process of counselling her, the Lord revealed a lot of things about her, principally in the areas where she had gone wrong. Based on the Lord's revelations, I rebuked her, and thereafter I prayed for her. Her husband no doubt did wrong her, by getting involved in an extramarital affair with another woman, who was their neighbour and was also using charm on both the man and the woman. As a result of the effect of the charm, she became estranged from the husband's relations leading to the breakdown of the marriage and subsequent separation from her husband for seven years.

Based on the message which I received from

the Lord, I told her that her husband's relations would become anxious for her to return to her husband. This was exactly what happened. It was not long she came back to tell me that after I prayed for her, whenever the husband's relations saw her, they would ask her, 'When are you coming back?' This continued for a while, because she did not believe that they meant it, because they so hated her and never wanted to see her around. When she came back to recount her experience, I reminded her that the Holy Spirit does not lie, and encouraged her to return to her husband. Naturally, she was apprehensive; having separated for seven years which was quite a long time. However she strengthened herself and returned to her matrimonial home and was received with arms open.

A Girl Delivered From A Lying Spirit

The devil will stop at nothing in its attempt to make a believer miserable; he will even use your own child to torment you. This was exactly what he did to a woman who came to me in tears. When asked what her problem was, she narrated the ordeal which her daughter, about six years old, was putting her through. This happened in the presence of the girl. As we talked, she introduced the girl as her daughter; but right in my presence, the girl denied being her daughter. The woman was so embarrassed and close to tears, and told me that, that was what she usually did to her. Even in her place of business (the woman was a trader), her daughter would always embarrass her and make her look as though she had stolen someone else's child. I enquired from the girl to confirm her relationship with the woman, and she insisted that the woman was not her mother. However, I decided to pray for them; and to my surprise and shock, after the prayer, the girl confessed that the woman was her mother. This is how wicked the devil can be.

The woman was very thankful and told me that as they came closer to my house, while coming, the girl refused to continue the journey, and that it took a long while to persuaded her to follow her. The reason for her reluctance being as the Holy Spirit revealed to me, the demons in her had known that they would be cast out, which would lead to the girl being delivered.

A Couple Got Married After Many Years Of Futile Attempts

A couple had been trying to get married to each other for years but were hindered by the enemy, the devil. They came to me for prayer, and after the prayer, the Lord removed the obstacle. they got married within weeks and have been happily married ever since.

A Barren Woman Gave Birth To A Child After Eighteen Years Of Fruitless Marriage

Yes, this really happened. During a house fellowship meeting; the Lord led me to pray for people, and the woman in question was in the meeting, and I prayed for her because I knew that she had a problem in her marriage, which was childlessness. After I prayed for her by God's grace, she became pregnant within the very season and subsequently gave birth to a baby boy. To God be the glory.

There are so many testimonies of what the Lord has done in my ministry, which time will not permit me to enumerate all of them here. Those will form the subjects of another book in the future.

Healing Of A Hunchback Woman

There was this lady in my work place, who always looked very fierce and dreadful; people always avoided her except if they had some important assignment to carry out in her office. She was always hostile to fellow staff. One day, I had the urge to go and minister the Word of God to her but hadn't enough courage, so I appealed to a sister colleague to accompany me, but she was reluctant. However, after much pleading, But as soon as we entered into the woman's office, she changed her mind again and left me all alone there. As soon as we entered the woman's office, she ran changed her mind and left me all alone there. I nearly left as well, one would need a lot of courage to be with the woman in question. In any case, I stayed on and told her why I was there; she almost refused to listen to me, but I persisted, and in the end, she yielded and eventually gave her life to Christ. A few weeks later, something happened, a miracle had taken place. Her hunchback had completely disappeared, and she was now more beautiful and friendly. To God be the glory, Hallelujah.

A Girl Delivered From The Hands Of Death

My little grandniece narrowly escaped death, because of God's intervention. It happened two days after her first birthday. That day, I visited my sister earlier in the day, but as I was driving back from work that late afternoon, a soft voice said to me,' 'Go to so address, which happened to be my sister's address, then I thought to myself, 'But I was there earlier in the day.' But the voice repeated the instruction. At this point, I realised that it was the Lord talking to me. Then I headed to the address. As soon as I entered the house, to my surprise, I saw the child on the shoulder of her grandmother (my sister), and I observed that the girl was pale-grey and looking lifeless, and my sister looking terribly confused. I immediately carried the girl from her and prayed a simple and short prayer, rebuking the spirit of death; suddenly, the child regained consciousness. I am not sure I told my sister that the Spirit of God instructed me to come back, because she was too confused. The parents of the girl had gone to work. This was a child who had her first birthday two days earlier. I only thank God for instructing me to go back there.

Healing Of A Sick Woman Who Was Taken To A Healing Church But To No Avail

This woman was taken to a popular healing church for healing, but after five weeks there, there was no visible improvement. But the husband who happened to be my colleague in the office came into my office in tears to narrate his ordeal, then I prayed for her and God healed her instantly and she was brought back home.

Many Children And Adults Received Their Healing, Even Some That Defied Medical Solutions

God wrought many miracles carrying out healings in my family and that of my relations.' Families were delivered from the spirit of poverty. A man who could not occupy his office after he was promoted to a senior position, even after he was prayed for by many other senior ministers, was able to occupy his office after I prayed for him through his wife.

God of Miracle

Hear the testimony of a renowned man of God, whose name I would prefer not to mention. He said that at one time in his ministry, as a result of his preaching, some men confronted him and his team while armed with AK47 guns. He looked at them and prayed in his mind, and the men went away defeated, unable to carry out their evil operation, because of the power in the name of the Lord Jesus Christ. This is proof that prayer does not have to be audible.

Again, here is another testimony from another man of God. It is about how armed robbers came to kill him in his office, again with a gun, and he merely said to them, 'Your gun perish with you' And immediately they fled. Oh dear, what authority we have in the name of Jesus as believers! This is the God that I am introducing to you. Get to know Him, and you will never remain the same again.

CHAPTER THIRTY

The Beginning of My Ministry

WHEN THE LORD called me into the ministry in 1988 in the dream. But launched me out in 1990, when He gave me a message which He asked me to deliver to the Full Gospel Business Men's Fellowship in Port Harcourt, in Nigeria, where Brother Douglas who was then Commissioner for Information, was an executive member at the time. This message was delivered during their Musical Night of that year, and the Lord took the glory because many evangelical ministries and fellowships erupted as a result of that message.

The praying Ministry started in 1997, and I started by praying for all the states in my country (Nigeria), especially all the south-south and south-eastern states, because this is where I am from. It was not long after I started praying this prayer, that I began to hear that states like Abia, followed by many others were now having prayer sessions during their working hours, in the government's offices. The practice spread to other states. I am not here trying to take all the glory. I know other servants and children of God might have been praying also.

Of course, this was preceded by the Rivers State, during the Governorship of Rufus Ada George. He started a Christian fellowship in the Government House, and thanks to Bishop Elkanah Hanson, who was then a Senior Pastor of Elshadai Bible Church, which the Governor attended. Bishop Hanson led Governor Adah George to Christ in 1991/92.

In early 1991, the Lord told me to establish a fellowship at my work place. And in early 1992, I was sent to the Administrative Staff College of Nigeria (ASCON) in Badagry near Lagos, on a short course. While at ASCON, and to my surprise, I met Brother Douglas is the same as brother Bernard at the cafeteria; who was also there for a course. In course of conversation, he said to me, 'Sister, do you know that in our state [that is, Rivers State], staff cannot start work at the State Secretariat Complex without having a prayer session? And this applies to all the ministries.' I was very surprised, then I responded, 'Really? You don't mean it.' And as soon as I said that, the Lord said to me, 'Now you have no excuse.' Thereafter I remembered what He had told me about establishing a fellowship at my work place some time ago, but I was afraid because at that time, having Christian fellowship in a workplace was not conventional. Following the above information, I was able to established a Fellowship in July 1992 known as "The Redeemed Civil Servants' Fellowship. For more details on prayer and types of prayer, please visit the chapter on various types of prayer, where more details are made available on the subject.

There is no limit to the number of problems we can solve through prayer. Sometimes, we forget to go to God in prayer, but would rather sit and brood over our problems rather than meditate on the Word of God or take our problems to the Lord.

CHAPTER THIRTY-ONE

Men and Women of God Who Excelled Through Prayer

Part 1- V

Part I

T HE CONCEPT OF prayer did not start with us but right in the Bible, many centuries ago. And was therefore written for us to learn from. In the Bible, we read of men and women of God who excelled through prayer; such people like Jabez, Paul, and Silas, Esther, Nehemiah, Daniel, Peter, Hannah, and many others. Jesus Himself never stopped praying when He was on earth; it is important that we follow His example, because that was one of the reasons why His Father sent Him into the world, to come and teach us how to fight our spiritual battles, among other things. Let us therefore learn from the following men and women of God and their experiences.

Jabez

Jabez's Prayer

The name Jabez means sorrow. The Bible lets us

know that Jabez was more honourable (had great respect) than his brothers, and his mother called his name J abez, saying Because I bare him with sorrow' (pain). Parents should be careful in choosing the type of name they give to their children. Jabez was a descendant of Judah. In faith, he held unto God and sought his blessing and that faith triumphed, for God granted what he desired And J abez called on the God of Israel saying: "Oh that you would bless me indeed and enlarge my territory, that Your hand would be with me, and that you would keep me from evil, that I may not cause pain' (!Chronicles 4:9-10 NKJV). So God granted him what he requested.

Jacob

Jacob Wrestled With An Angel

It is neither an easy nor a cheap thing to have an encounter with an angel, but Jacob always did. It takes a praying child of God to have experience with an angel; even at that, it is still neither easy nor common. Prayer can change your situation. Jacob's destiny was changed when God changed his name from Jacob to Israel. Let us see his experiences:

An Angel Wrestled With Jacob In The Night As He Slept

After Jacob served his uncle Laban, he decided to go away, taking with him his wives, Leah and Rachel.

'And he arose that night, took his two wives, his two female servants, and his eleven sons, and crossed over the ford of Jabbok. He took and sent them over the brook, and sent over, what he had. Then Jacob was left alone; and a man wrestled with him until the break of day. Now when he saw that he did not prevail against him, he touched the socket of Jacob's hip; and the socket of Jacob hip was out of joint as he wrestled with him. And he said, 'Let Me go, for the day breaks.' But he said, 'I will not let you go unless You bless me!' So He said to him, 'What is your name?' He said, acob.' And He said, 'Your name shall no longer be called Jacob, but Israel, for you have struggled with God and with men, and have prevailed.' Then Jacob asked, saying, 'Tell me Your name, I pray.' And He said, 'Why is it that you ask about my name?' And He blessed him there.

So Jacob called the name of the place Peniel: 'For I have seen God face to face, and my life is preserved." He said so because no one who sees God's face ever lives, even though from experience God can reveal Himself to whosoever He wishes and such revelation can take any form.'

As Jacob left the place after he had the encounter with the angel of God, something happened: 'Just as he crossed over to Peniel the sun rose on him, and he limped on his hip. Therefore to this day the children of Israel do not eat the muscle that shrank, which is on the hip socket, because he [the angel] touched the socket of Jacob's hip in the muscle that shrank' (Gen. 32:29-32 NKJV).

Having considered Jacob's, one cannot help wondering if Jacob ever recovered from the effect of that incident. He may have limped till his death.

As stated earlier, God did not appear to Jacob only once; as a result of his prayer life, the Lord appeared to him again: Then God appeared to Jacob again, when he came from Patlan Aram and blessed him. And God said to him, 'Your name is Jacob, your name shall not be called Jacob anymore, but Israel shall be your name.' So his name was changed to Israel, (Gen. 35:9-10 NKJV). That was a confirmation that his name had really changed.

Prayer draws us closer to our Creator and enables us to maintain a cordial relationship with Him based on our obedience to His Word.

Abraham

Abraham would not have become a friend of God if he had not been prayerful. It takes a prayerful Christian to exercise faith and to believe in God's promises. We are taught in the Bible that Abraham believed God, and it was accounted unto him for righteousness. Abraham was able to wait for twenty-five years for Isaac to be born, after the Lord God promised that He would give him a son. This is a clear manifestation of obedience and long-suffering.

Moses

Moses could not have delivered the children of Israel successfully to the promised land if he had not been a prayerful servant of God. God started by revealing Himself to Moses at Mount Horeb. Thereafter, the Lord God sent him to Pharaoh, where He used him to perform wonders in Pharaoh's palace. The life of Moses was full of interactions with God, and this included Moses staying in the presence of God for forty days and forty nights, after which he received the Ten Commandments of God for mankind among other things. Moses did not only pray for the children of Israel; he defended them.

Jacobed

This woman was Moses' mother. She was the daughter of Levi, Amram. Something tells me that this woman was a woman of prayer. She was also bold, and this is evidenced in the fact that babies were being killed. When she could no longer hide her son in the house, she conceived I the idea of putting him in an ark of bulrushes (papyrus basket), daubed it with asphalt and pitch, and dropped him by the bank of River Nile. Moses' sister (Miriam), willingly waited, not being sure what would happen, but by God's own divine intervention, Pharaoh's daughter came to bathe in the Nile River at that time. God also gave Miriam, the boldness and wisdom to recommend to the daughter of Pharaoh a nurse for the baby.

God works in mysterious ways. It takes a prayerful child of God to be sensitive in the spirit. Jacobed did not know what assignment God had created his son for, not to talk of knowing that he was the one God would use to deliver the children of Israel from their afflictions. (See also Exod. 2:1-5 NIV, footnote.)

Part II

Nehemiah

The name Nehemiah means "Comfort of Yahweh." He was one of the children of Israel who were captured during the captivity and carried to Babylon. He led the third and the last return to Jerusalem, after the Babylonian exile. While in captivity he was a cupbearer to the king of Persia, Artaxerzes. Nehemiah was also a man of God who excelled through prayer because of concern for his people, after their captivity.

Before we discuss Nehemiah's prayer life, a little light needs to be on what transpired which led him to pray, and what he did before, during, and after he prayed. Nehemiah was the son of Hachaliah. He was a Jew and was a cupbearer to the king of Persia, King Artaxerxes. Nehemiah was a ruler of half a district of Jerusalem before the captivity.

The Captivity of Israelites

It will be recalled that Jeremiah the Prophet prophesied concerning the captivity of the children of Israel as a result of their disobedience to their God.

Jeremiah's Prophecy

The word that came to Jeremiah concerning all the people of Judah in the fourth year of Jehoiakim, the son of Josiah, king of Judah, that was the first year of Nebuchadrezar, king of Babylon. The word which Jeremiah the prophet spake unto all the inhabitants of Jerusalem, saying, 'From the thirteenth year of Josiah, the son of Amon, king of Judah, even unto this day, that is the three and twentieth year, the word of the Lord had come unto me, and I have spoken unto you, rising early and speaking; but ye have not hearkened. And the Lord hath sent unto you all the servants, the prophets, rising early and sending them; but ye have not hearkened, nor inclined your ear to hear. They said, Turn ye again now everyone from his evil way, and from the evil of your doings, and dwell in the land that the Lord hath given unto you and to your fathers for ever and ever.

And go not after other gods to serve them, and to worship them, and provoked me not to anger with the works of your hands; and I will do you no hurt. Yet ye have not hearkened unto me, saith -the Lord; that ye might provoke me to anger with the works of your hands to your own hurt.

For many nations and great kings shall serve themselves of then also: and I will recompense them according to their deeds, and according to the works of their own hands.

For thus saith the Lord God of Israel unto me; 'Take the wine cup of the fury of my hand, and cause all the nations, to whom I send thee, to drink it.'

And they shall drink and be moved and be mad, because of the sword that I will send among them. Jeremiah did even as the Lord commanded.

'Then took I the cup at the Lord's hand, and made all the nations to drink, unto whom the Lord had sent me.'

Therefore thus saith the Lord of hosts; because ye have not heard my words. Behold, I will send and take all the families of the north, saith the Lord, and Nebuchadrezar king of Babylon, my servant, and will bring them against this land, and against all these nations round about, and will utterly destroy them, and make them an astonishment and an hissing, and perpetual desolations.

Moreover, I will take from them the voice of mirth, and voice of gladness, the voice of the bridegroom, and the voice of the bride, the sound of the millstones, and light of the candle. And this whole land shall be a desolation, and an astonishment, and this nation shall serve the king of Babylon seventy years ... ' The Lord also promised to punish the king of Babylon, and that nation, for their iniquity, and the land of the Chaldeans, and make it perpetual desolation. And will bring upon their land all His words which He had pronounced against it, even all that is written in this book [the Bible], which Jeremiah had prophesied against the nations.

May I say that the nations in turmoil today namely, Assyria, which is now known as Syria today, and other Arab countries are in their predicament because of this prophecy? The word of God never goes unfulfilled. This is the reason why we should fear the Lord by observing His commands.

These nations mentioned in the Book of Jeremiah 25:19-26, include:

Egypt, Uz, Ashkelon, Azzah, and Ekron, and the remnant of Ashdod, Edam and Moab and the children of Amon. Also mentioned are - And all the kings of Tyrus, the kings of Zidon, the kings of the Isle which are beyond the sea.

Deddan and Terna, and Buz, and all that are in the uttermost corners. Also all the kings of Arabia, and all the kings of mingled people that dwell in the desert . . . And all the kings of the north far and near, and all the kingdoms of the world, which are upon the face of the earth: and the king of Sheshach shall drink after them, as the Lord said.

Therefore thou shall say unto them, Thus saith the Lord of hosts, the God of Israel; Drink ye, and be drunken, and spue, and fall, and rise no more, because of the sword which I will send among you. And it shall be, if they refuse to take the cup at thine hand to drink, then shalt thou say unto them, Thus says the Lord of hosts; Ye shall certainly drink.'

Please read Jeremiah 25 for full details.

Jeremiah prophesied again to the people of Judah and to all those living in Jerusalem concerning their hardheartedness and disobedience to God's command, and said: 'For twenty-three years from the thirteenth year of Josiah son of Amon, King of Judah until this very day, the word of the Lord has come to me and I have spoken to you again and again, but you have not listened.'

I took time to quote this passage because I want you to see why the Lord was angry with the people of Israel. Again I will like you to note that God never punished a people without forewarning them.

As a result of the continuous disobedience of the people of Judah in Jerusalem and their refusal to heed to God's warnings, God caused them to be taken into captivity and for the Babylonians to destroy the walls of Jerusalem and also break their gates. All these happened in fulfilment of Gods' warnings.

In the book of Ezra, the Lord spoke to King Cyrus concerning what he wanted him to do regarding the rebuilding of Judah in Jerusalem:

> Now in the first year of Cyrus, king of Persia, that the Word of the Lord by the mouth of Jeremiah might be fulfilled, the Lord stirred up the spirit of Cyrus King of Persia that he made a proclamation throughout all his kingdom, and put it also in writing, saying: Thus says Cyrus the King of Persia. The Lord God of heaven hath given me all the Kingdom of the earth; and he hath charged me to build him an house at Jerusalem, which is in Judah. Who is there among all his people? His God be with him, and let him go up to Jerusalem, which is in Judah, and build the house of the Lord God of Israel, (He is the God,) which is in Jerusalem. And whosoever remaineth in any

place where he sojourneth, let the men of his place help him with silver and with gold, and with goods, beasts, beside the freewill offering for the house of God that is in Jerusalem. (Ezra 1:1-4 KJV).

Nehemiah Receives News Of Destruction Of Jerusalem

Nehemiah was in the king's palace a message came to him through one of his brethren, Hanani, and brought him bad news about Jerusalem, telling him how the walls of Jerusalem were broken down.

It came to pass in the month of Chislev, in the twentieth year, as I was in Shushan the citadel, that Hanani, one of my brethren, came with (certain) men from Judah; and I asked them concerning the Jews who had escaped, who had survived the captivity and concerning Jerusalem. And they said to me, 'The survivors who are left from the captivity in the province are there in great distress and reproach. The wall of Jerusalem is also broken down, and its gates are burned with fire.' (Neh. 1:1-3 KJV)

Nehemiah's Reaction And Prayer

So it was, when I heard these words, that I sat down and wept, and mourned for many days; I was fasting and praying before the God of heaven. (Neh. 1:1-4 KJV)

"O great and awesome God .." You who keep your covenant and mercy with those who love you and observe your commandments. Please let your ear be attentive and your eyes open, that you may hear the prayer of your servant which I pray before you now, day and night, for the children of Israel your servants, and confess the sins of the children of Israel which we have sinned against You. Both my father's house and I have sinned. We have acted very corruptly against You, and have not kept the commandments, the statutes, nor the ordinances which You commanded your servant Moses.

Nate that Nehemiah never excluded himself from the sins of his people, by claiming self-righteousness.

Now these are your servants and your people. Whom You have redeemed by Your great power, and by Your strong hand. Oh Lord I pray let Your ear be attentive to the prayer of your servant, and to the prayer of your servants who desire to fear your name; and let your servant prosper this day, I pray, and grant him mercy in the sight of this man.

Nehemiah here referred to the king in Shushan, King Artaxerxes: 'For I was the king's cupbearer.'

Nehemiah Reminded God What Led To The Captivity

Remember, I pray, the word that You commanded your servant Moses, saying, 'If you are unfaithful I will scatter you among the nations: but if you return to me and keep My commandments and do them, though some of you were cast out to the farthest part of the heavens, yet I will gather them from there, and bring them to the place which I have chosen as a dwelling for my name' (Neh. 1:8-9 NKJV)

Notice from the above that the Lord had already destined Jerusalem to be His dwelling place.

Did God answer Nehemiah's prayer? Of course He did. Not only did the king grant him his request, the Lord God gave him favour with King Artaxerxes, who helped him to procure all that he needed with which to rebuild Jerusalem.

The emphasis here is importance of prayer. Nehemiah was able to receive favour from the king as a result of his effectual and fervent prayer. Prayer is the answer to all problems. If you read chapters 2 and 3 of the book of Nehemiah, you will see what transpired as a result of Nehemiah's prayer.

Part III

Esther

Esther is an epitome of a praying Christian. Esther excelled as a prayer warrior whom God used in delivering her people, the Jews, from the evil plan of Haman during the reign of King Ahasuerus, who reigned over a hundred and twenty provinces. She was also a model for believers who were fervent in their prayer life. It may be important to examine what Esther did and what led to the things she did.

There was this king whose name was Ahasuerus; he was the ruler of India as well as Ethiopia. He had a wife who was his queen, and her name was Queen Vashti. It happened that in the third year of the his reign, he arranged a feast for all his princes and his servants, and the people of Persia and Media and all the nobles were before him. After this, the king also organized a feast for all the people that were in Shushan in the palace. Also, Queen Vashti made a feast for the women in the royal house.

Queen Vashti's Disobedience And Punishment

Then towards the end of the whole ceremony, the king was in a high mood as he had drunk wine, he ordered that Queen Vashti be brought before him with the royal crown so that he could show her to the people because she was beautiful to look upon. But Queen Vashti refused to come out at the King's command, and the king was wroth, and enquired of all his wise men and all those in a position of authority within the province what should be done to Queen Vashti. One of the princes, named Memucan, suggested that the king make a royal commandment in writing stating that Vashti came no more before the king and that the king should give her royal estate to another that was better than her, for disobeying the king's commandment in order that other women might not disrespect their husbands. The king did not hesitate to carry out this suggestion. This was how Queen Vashti lost her estate. God dethrones one and enthrones another. This is how the Lord God will turn things around in your favour, simply because you are reading this book.

How the Lord Lifted Esther (Esther 1-2)

After Queen Vashti may have lost her royal estate, the king's servant suggested to the king that 'fair young virgins be sought for the king, and let the maiden which pleases the king be queen instead of Vashti.'

In the Shushan palace, there was a man named Mordecai, who was a Jew; he was the son of J air, a descendant of the Kish, a Benjamite. Mordecai I had been carried away from Jerusalem during the captivity which had been carried away with Jeconiah, king of Judah, whom Nebuchadnezzar, the king of Babylon, had carried away.

Then Mordecai brought Esther, whose name was Hadasah at the time, and she was Mordecai's uncle's daughter and was an orphan because she had neither mother nor father. This was how Esther, who was a Jew, was picked, because she pleased the king and she obtained kindness from him, and so Esther was made queen. Someone's disappointment may turn out to be your blessing as God remembers you through your prayer and obedience to His Word.

Haman Promoted

In those days while Mordecai sat within the king's gate, two of the king's eunuchs or chamberlains, by name Bigthana and Teresh, doorkeepers, became furious and sought to lay hands on the king. And the matter was made known to Mordecai, who mentioned it to Esther, who also informed the king, in Mordecai's name. As a result of this plot, the two men were hanged. This was written in the book of remembrance known as the book of Chronicles, in the presence of King Ahasuerus.

Haman Plotted To Destroy The Jews

And it came to pass that after these things, Haman the son of Hammedatha, the Agagite, was promoted and advanced and set his seat above all the princes who were with him. And all the king's servant within the palace began to bow down and even paid homage to Haman, for so the king had commanded concerning him. But as the Bible recorded, Mordecai refused to pay homage to Haman; the reason that Mordecai gave was Jews only bow down to God and not to men. As a result of Mordecai's disobedience of the king's command, Haman became wroth with Mordecai and planned to destroy all the Jews who were throughout the whole kingdom.

Then Haman reported the Jews to the king and said, 'There is a certain scattered and dispersed among the people in all the provinces of your kingdom; their laws are different from all other peoples, and they do not keep the king's laws. Therefore, it is not fitting for the king to let them remain. If it pleases the king, let a decree be written that they be destroyed, and I will pay ten thousand talents of silver into the hands of those who do the work to bring it into the king's treasuries.' And the king said to Haman, 'The money and the people are given to you, to do with them as seems good to you.' Then the decree was written according to all that Haman commanded, in various languages, in the name of King Ahasuerus and was sealed with the king's signet ring and sent to all the provinces. And Haman went to his house and began to celebrate, but the city of Shushan was perplexed.

Mordecai's Reaction (Esther 4:1 Nkjv)

When Mordecai heard what Haman had planned, he tore his clothes and put on sackcloth and ashes, and went out into the midst of the city and cried a loud and bitter cry. He went as far as the king's gate, for no one might enter the king's gate clothed with sackcloth. All the Jews went into mourning, fasting, weeping, and wailing when they heard of Haman's plot, and many lay in sackcloth and ashes. And Esther was told.

So Esther's maids and eunuchs came and told her, and the queen was deeply distressed. Then she sent garments to clothe Mordecai and took his sackcloth away from him, but he would not accept them. This made Esther became curious, and she moved to enquire why. Then Esther sent one of her eunuchs to find out from Mordecai who was in front of the king's gate, and Mordecai' told all that had happened to him and the sum of money that Haman had promised to pay into the king's treasuries to destroy the Jews. He also gave him a copy of the written decrees for their destruction, which was given at Shushan, to show it to Esther with explanation. Mordecai also told him to tell Esther to make supplication to the king and plead before him for the Jews.

Esther's Response

This was Esther's response. I quote: Then Esther spoke to Hat Hach, and gave him a command for Mordecai. 'All the king's servants and the people of the king's provinces know that any man or woman who goes into the inner court to the king, who has not been called, he has but one law; put all to death, except the one to whom the king holds out the golden sceptre, that he may live. Yet I myself have not been called to go into the king these thirty days.' (Esther 4:11 NKJV)

It is not surprising that Esther was afraid of the king, because she saw what happened to Queen Vashti. When they told Mordecai Esther's response, Mordecai told them to answer Esther thus: 'Do not think in your heart that you will escape in the king's palace any more than all the other Jews. For if you remain completely silent at this time, relief and deliverance will arise for the Jew from another place, but you and your father's house will perish. Yet who knows whether you have come to the kingdom for such a time as this?'

Queen Esther's Intervention

Then Esther told them to reply to Mordecai, 'Go gather all the Jews who are present in Shushan, and fast for me; neither eat nor drink for three days, night or day. My maids and I will fast likewise. And so I will go to the king, which is against the law; and if I perish, I perish' (Esther 4:16 NKJV). So Mordecai did even as Esther had commanded him.

On the third day of the fast, Esther went in to see the king in her royal robes and stood in the inner court of the palace. And when the king saw her standing in the court, and immediately the king held out to Esther his golden sceptre that was in his hand. Then Esther went near and touched the top of the sceptre, this signifying the fact that the king had welcomed her. Then the king enquired of her what the matter was. And the king said to her, What do you wish, Queen Esther? What is your request? It shall be given to you up to half the kingdom!' This is what fasting and prayer can do. God uses it to fight for us, and ultimately give us victory. Note how the king was moved to promise Esther even up to the half of his kingdom.

Esther answered, 'If it pleases the king, let the king and Haman come today to the banquet that I have prepared for him.' Then the king said, 'Bring Haman quickly, that he may do as Esther has said.' So the king and Haman went to the banquet that Esther had prepared. The king did not waste time to know why Esther prepared the banquet, so at the banquet of wine, which is even before the main banquet, the king asked, 'What is your petition, up to half of the kingdom? It shall be done!'

Then Esther narrated her complaint: 'If I have found favour in the sight of the king, and if it pleases the king to grant my petition and fulfil my request, then let the king and Haman come to the banquet which I will prepare for them, and tomorrow I will do as the king has said.' (Esther 5:1-8 NKJV)

Haman's Pride Destroyed Him

Esther's invitation sent Haman celebrating before time; he went and . invited his friends and his wife Zeresh, telling them how highly placed he was: the king's promotion and the queen's invitation to her banquet, his riches, the multitude of his children, and all the rest of it. Then he said, 'Yet all this avails me nothing, so long as I see Mordecai the Jew sitting at the king's gate.' Then his wife Zeresh and all his friends said to him, 'Let gallows be made, fifty cubits high, and in the morning suggest to the king that Mordecai be hanged on it: then go merrily with the king to the banquet.' And the thing pleased Haman; so he had the gallows made.' (Esther 5:9-14 NKJV)

God Had Started Answering Esther's And The Jews' Prayer

The king was so troubled that sleep left his eyes that night, so much that he decided to do something; read and see what happened.

That night it is reported that the king could hardly sleep and commanded that the book of records be brought: 'That night the king could not sleep. So one was commanded to bring the books of records of chronicles: and they were before the king. And it was found written that Mordecai had told of Bigthana and Teresh, two of the king's eunuchs, the doorkeepers who had sought to lay hands on King Ahasuerus. Then the king said, 'What honour or dignity has been bestowed on Mordecai for this?' And the king's servants who attended him said, 'Nothing has been done for him.' (Esther 6:1-3 NKJV)

Mordecai's Promotion

This is very interesting, as Haman came into the king's court to tell the king to hang Mordecai on the gallows he had prepared for him. Before Haman could open his mouth, the king asked him, 'What shall be done for the man whom the king delights to honour?

Of course, Haman thought he was the one that the king wanted to honour, and thought in his heart: Whom would the king delight to honour more than me? So he answered and said to the king: Let a royal robe be brought which the king had worn, and a horse on which the king had ridden, which has a royal crest placed on its head. Then let this robe and horse be delivered to the hand of one of the king's most noble princes, that he may array the man whom the king delights to honour. Then parade him on horseback through the city square and proclaim before him: 'Thus shall it be done to the man whom the king delights to honour!'

Then the king said to Haman, 'Hurry, take the robe and the horse, as you have suggested, and do so for Mordecai the Jew who sits within the king's gate! Leave nothing undone of all that you have spoken.' Immediately, Haman did as the king commanded. So Haman took the robe and the horse, and arrayed Mordecai and led him on horseback through the city square, and proclaimed before him, 'Thus shall it be done to the man whom the king delights to honour!' Afterwards, Mordecai went back to the king's gate. But

Haman hurried to his house mourning and with his head covered.

When Haman told his wife Zeresh and all his friends everything that had happened to him, his wise men and his wife Zeresh said to him, 'If Mordecai before whom you have begun to fall is of Jewish descent, you will not prevail against him, but will surely fall before him.' While they were still talking with him, the king's eunuchs came, and hastened to bring Haman to the banquet which Esther had prepared.

As the king and Haman went to dine with Queen Esther, on the second day the king asked Esther, 'What is your petition, Queen Esther? It shall be granted you. And what is your request, up to half of the kingdom? It shall be done.' May I suggest that every woman should earnestly and prayerfully covet the wisdom of Esther?

Then Queen Esther answered, 'If I have found favour in your sight, 0 king, and if it pleases the king, let my life be given me at my petition, and my people at my request. For we have both been sold, people and I, to be destroyed, to be killed, and to be annihilated. Had we been sold as male and female slaves, I would have held my tongue, although the enemy could never compensate for the king's loss.'

As Esther uttered the above, King Ahasuerus answered and said to Queen Esther, 'Who is he, and where is he, who will dare to presume such a thing in his heart to do such a thing?'

Then Esther said, 'The adversary and the enemy

is this wicked Haman!' At this, Haman became terrified before the king and the queen. Then the king arose in his wrath from the banquet of wine and went into the palace garden, but Haman stood before Queen Esther, pleading for his life, for he saw that evil was determined against him by the king.

When the King returned from the palace garden to the place of the banquet of wine, Haman had fallen across the couch where Esther was. Then the king said, 'Will he also assault the queen while I am in the house?' As the words left the king's mouth, they covered Haman's face.

Now comes the boomerang: As the above happened, one of king's eunuchs, named Harbonah, said to the king, 'Look! The gallows fifty cubits high, which Haman made for Mordecai, who spoke good on the king's behalf is standing at the house of Haman.'

Then the king said, 'Hang him on it.' (Esther 6:6-7:9 NKJV)

This was how Haman was hung on the gallows that he made for Mordecai. This was a wonderful deliverance for the Jewish people. This is what the Lord will do to your enemies because you are reading this book. Remember that this victory was achieved through prayer and faith in God.

Part IV

Hannah

There was a man of Romathaim Zophim, of the mountain of Ephraim whose name was Elkanah. Elkanah had two wives the name of one was Hannah and the name of the other was Peninnah. Hannah was barren but Peninnah had children. As a result of Hannah's barrenness, Peninnah began to mock her.

It was the custom of Elkanah to go from his city yearly to worship and sacrifice to the Lord in a place called Shiloh. During the sacrifice, and whenever it was time for Elkanah to make an offering he would give portions to Peninnah his wife and to all her sons and daughters. But to Hannah he would give a double portion, for he loved Hannah, though she was barren. And Peninnah her rival also provoked her severely, according to the Bible, to make her miserable because the Lord had   closed her womb. This happened every year each time they went to the house of the Lord, her rival Peninnah would provoke her; as a result Hannah wept, and refused to eat.

Hannah Prayed To God For A Child

She arose after they had finished eating and drinking in Shiloh one day. She went to the tabernacle of the Lord, where Eli the priest was sitting by the doorpost. She was so bitter in her soul she prayed to the Lord and wept in anguish. And she made a vow and said, 'O Lord of hosts, if You will indeed look on the affliction of Your maidservant and remember me, and not forget Your maidservant, but will give Your maidservant a male child, then I will give him to the Lord all the days of his life, and no razor shall come upon his head.'

When Eli watched and saw her but did not know what she was saying, because she was praying in her heart, Eli thought that she was drunk. And Eli told her, 'Put your wine away from you!'

But Hannah answered and said, 'No, my lord, I am a woman of sorrowful spirit, I have drunk neither wine nor intoxicating drink, but have poured out my soul before the Lord. Do not consider your maidservant a wicked woman, for out of the abundance of my complaint and grief I have spoken until now.'

Then Eli answered, 'Go in peace, and the God of Israel grant your petition which you have asked of Him.'

And she said, 'Let your maidservant find favour in your sight.' So Hannah went her way and ate, and her face was no longer sad. (1 Sam. 1:1-18 NKJV)

God Answered Hannah's Prayer

So it came to pass in the process of time that Hannah conceived and bore a son and called his name Samuel, saying, 'Because I have asked for him from the Lord.' (1 Sam. 1: 20 NKJV)

Again, the Lord showed Himself a prayer

answering God. Hannah, who was barren has now become the mother of Samuel. This is a lesson to always take your problems to God in prayer.

Peter

Peter's Prayer Life

Peter prayed until he saw a vision of an open heaven, and an object like great sheet bound at the four corners, descending to him and let down to the earth in which were all kinds of four footed animals of the earth, wild beasts, creeping things, and birds of the air. And a voice came to him, 'Rise, Peter, kill and eat.' (Acts 10 NKJV)

Peter was another disciple of Jesus Christ who was always praying.

It was in course of Peter's prayer that the Lord gave him a vision which led him to go to minister to Cornelius. Peter was the disciple who took the gospel to a Gentile nation. It was through prayer that the Lord sent Peter to minister to Cornelius. Cornelius was in Caesarea, he was also a centurion in what was the Italian Regiment. Cornelius was the first Gentile man to receive the gospel of Christ.

Prayer Wrought Wonders In The Life Of Peter

It was also the prayer of brethren that caused Peter to be released from prison miraculously (Acts 12).

Daniel

Daniel was one of the men of God in the Bible who received answers to his prayer. Although the enemy tried to delay it by intercepting it, the answer was released to him eventually, because he was a man of prayer. Daniel prayed so much to his God that his enemies became very uncomfortable and plotted against him but could not find a way except in his prayer life, because he was always praying.

Daniel was another man of God whose life as depicted in the Bible is worth emulating. His exemplary spiritual life included prayer, vision, dreams and interpretation, prophetic gift, humility. Even when he was thrown into the lion's den, he still remained humble. Daniel's life and ministry cover the entire seventy-year period of Babylonian captivity. Deported to Babylon at the age of sixteen and handpicked for government service, he became God's prophetic mouthpiece to the Gentile and Jewish world, declaring God's present and eternal purpose.

As a result of his steadfastness in worshiping his God, his enemies influenced King Nebuchadnezzar to make a decree against anyone who would not bow down to his image; nonetheless, Daniel remained faithful to his God and refused to bow to King Nebuchadnezzar's image. Hence, he was thrown into the fiery furnace. God gave him a great victory along with his brethren Shadrach, Meshach, and Abednego (Daniel 3).

Daniel was described as a young man who had an excellent spirit -that is the Spirit of God.

The Captivity Proper, And How Daniel Went To The King's Palace

Please refer below how Daniel found himself serving in the palace of the king of Babylon, Nebuchadnezzar.

In the third year of the reign of Jehoiakim, king of Judah, Nebuchadnezzar king of Babylon came to Jerusalem and besieged it. And the Lord gave Jehoiakim king of Judah into his hand, with some of the articles of the house of God, which he carried into the land of Shinar to the house of his god; and he brought the articles into the treasure house of his god. Then the king instructed Asphenaz, the master of his eunuchs, to bring some of the children of Israel and some of the king's descendants and some of the nobles, young men in whom there were no blemish, but good-looking, gifted in all wisdom, possessing knowledge and quick to understand, who had ability to serve in the king's palace, and whom they might teach the language and literature of the Chaldeans. Among those chosen were Daniel, Hananiah, Mishael, Azariah. Their names were later changed as follows by the chief of the eunuchs: Daniel he gave the name of Belteshazar: to Hananiah he gave Shadrach; to Mishael he gave Meshach; and to Azariah he gave Abednego. The king appointed for them to serve a daily provision of the king's delicacies and of the wine which the king drank, But Daniel purposed in his heart that he would not defile himself. Daniel was prayerful and spiritually steadfast in the things of God; hence, God granted him favour and goodwill with the chief of the eunuchs. Daniel pleaded with the steward whom the chief of the eunuchs had set over him, Hananiah, Mishael, and Azariah, 'Please test your servants for ten days, and let them give us vegetables to eat and water to drink. Then let our appearance be examined before you, and the appearance of the young men who eat the portion of the king's delicacies; and as you see fit, so deal with your servants,' the steward consented.

The Bible lets us know that at the end of ten days, their appearance was better than those of the young men who ate the portion of the king's delicacies.

Now the king had given the chief of the eunuchs when to bring the young men in, as the king interviewed them, none was found like Daniel and his brethren; therefore, they were made to serve before the king. In all matters of wisdom and understanding about which the king examined them, they were found ten times better than all other magicians and astrologers who were in all the king's realm. As a result, Daniel was made to continue until the first year of King Cyrus, the next king after Nebuchadnezzar. This is what steadfastness in prayer can do. The Bible lets us know that they that knew their God would do exploits. Daniel was such a man (Daniel 1 NKJV).

Daniel's Promotion

The Lord so favoured Daniel that he had wisdom in other areas, including the area of dream interpretation, which earned Daniel promotion, when the Lord gave him wisdom to interpret the king's dream. He not only interpreted the king's dream, but also told the king's dream, which other astrologers and magicians could not do. In all these things, Daniel did not relent in the worship of his God.

Daniel's Prayer Life

Daniel prayed so much that when he was thrown into the lion's den, the Lord turned the lions into his friends, and they could not harm him.

As a result of Daniel's prayer life, God gave him favour before king Darius, who reigned after Cyrus. King Darius set over the kingdom one hundred and twenty satraps (a satrap was a governor of a province in ancient Persia). To be over the whole kingdom. These three governors of which Daniel was one, gave account to them, that the king might not suffer any loss. Again, Daniel distinguished himself above the governors and satraps, because an excellent spirit was in him (the spirit of God), so much that the king gave thought to setting him over the whole realm. As Daniel continued to be favoured by the Lord, the governors and the satraps sought to find some charge against Daniel concerning the kingdom but could find no charge or fault, because he was faithful; neither was there any error or fault found in him.

Plot Against Daniel

Because Daniel was always praying and faithful to his God, they decided to plot against him concerning the law of his God, by making the king sign a decree that no one should petition any god or man for thirty days except the king, or the person shall be cast into the den of lions. When Daniel knew that the writing was signed, he went home. And in his upper room, with his windows open toward Jerusalem, he knelt on his knees three times that day, and prayed, and gave thanks to his God, as was his custom since early days.

Then the men assembled and found Daniel praying and making supplications before his God. This was exactly the opportunity they were looking for. So they went to the king and reminded the king about his decree. 'Have you not signed a decree that every man who petitions any god or man within thirty days, except you, 0 king, shall be cast into the den of lions?'

The king answered, 'This is true, according to the law of Medes and Persians, which does not alter.'

Their plan had hatched. So they answered the king, 'That Daniel, who is one of the captives from Judah, does not show due regard for you,

0 King, nor for the decree that you have signed, makes his petition three times a day.'

Of course, what happened afterwards is a familiar story in the Bible. The king, on hearing this, was greatly displeased and set in his heart to deliver Daniel; he laboured till the going down of the sun.

When the men listened and heard nothing from the king, they went back to the king, and said to the king, 'Know, 0 king, that it is the law of the Medes and Persians that no decree or statute which the king establishes may be changed.' Observe how desperate these people were, incensed by the devil and enraged against Daniel. You know, I find this very interesting. Following their persistence, the king gave the command, and they brought Daniel and cast him into the den of lions.

But the king said to Daniel, 'Your God, whom you serve continually, He will deliver you.' Little did the king know that he was prophesying in Daniel's favour. Upon that, a stone was laid on the mouth of the den and sealed with king's signet ring and with signets of his lords, that no one might change their decision. Of course, the Lord delivered Daniel. Because instead of the lions having a feast on Daniel, the Lord caused the lions to become his friends.

King Darius came to find out about the fate of Daniel. The king, who could not sleep in the night because of fear of what might have happened to Daniel, even spent the night fasting and did not allow any musician to come to play for him, as was the custom in the palace.

God's Favour!

The king came very early in the morning to find out what might have happened to Daniel: Then the king arose very early in the morning and went in haste to the den of lions (imagine the love the King had for Daniel). And when he came to the den, he cried out with a lamenting voice to Daniel, 'Daniel, servant of the living God, has your God, whom you serve continually, been able to deliver you from the lions?'

Daniel, instead of exhibiting anger, exhibited the most humble nature that was in him, and replied to the king, 'O king, live forever! My God sent His angel and shut the lions' mouth so that they have not hurt me, because I was found innocent before Him, and so, 0 king, I have done no wrong before you.'

(Oh! The God that we serve is *the lion of the tribe of Judah*! What can He not do? He can do all things, of course.)

You would not believe it, the king was so glad: Now the king was exceeding glad for him and commanded that they should take Daniel up out of the den, so Daniel was taken up out of the den, and no injury whatever was found on him, because he believed in his God.

Now let us see what happened after: And the king gave the command, and they brought those men who had accused Daniel, and they cast them into the den of lions -them, their children, and their wives, and the lions overpowered them, and broke all their bones in pieces before they ever came to the bottom of the den. Wow, God of vengeance. Our God is a God that answers prayer. What can I say? It pays to live a life of prayer, brethren.

Now see what the king did after these things: *I make a decree that in every dominion of my kingdom) men must tremble and fear before the God of Daniel For He is the living God) and steadfast forever.*

His kingdom is the one which shall not be destroyed)

And His dominion shall endure till the end

He delivers and rescues, And He works signs and wonders, In heaven and on earth,

Who has delivered Daniel from the power of the lions

Again, I wish to state that this is the power of prayer (Daniel 6:1-27 NKJV).

This is how the Lord will deliver you from all those plotting against you, in Jesus' name.

Part V

Paul and Silas

Paul was a Judaic Jew, who persecuted the disciples of Jesus Christ. He went to the high priest and asked for letters from him to synagogues of Damascus, in order to bring anyone he would see on the way, be it men or women to Jerusalem bound. But as he journeyed, a light shone around him from heaven. As a result he fell on the ground and heard a voice saying to him: "Saul, Saul, why are you persecuting Me? " He answered and said, "Who are you Lord?" Then the voice said, "I am Jesus whom you are persecuting." It is hard for you to kick against the pricks." He trembling and astonished asked: Lord what do you have me to do? And the Lord said to him, "Arise and go into the city and you will be told what you must do." (Acts 9:1-5, KJV). After these things Saul who is also known as Paul, turned out to be the most effective apostle of Jesus Christ.

Paul had a vision in his dream, a man of Macedonia inviting him to come over and help them; he went with Silas, and later they stayed in Philippi, which was the foremost city in Macedonia. They stayed there for some days, and on the Sabbath day, they went out to the city by the riverside, where prayer was customarily made. After which they sat down and spoke to the women who they met there. In the course of their ministration, a woman whose name was Lydia, a seller of purple, from the city of Thyatira, who worshiped God, received the word spoken by Paul. As the Lord opened her heart to heed the things spoken by Paul, she and her household got baptised.

Paul And Silas Met By A Possessed Damsel

After these and all that followed, Paul and Silas

went to pray again. A certain slave girl who was possessed with the spirit of divination, who brought her masters much profit by fortune telling, met them and followed them and cried out, saying, 'These men are the servants f the Most High God, who proclaim to us the way of salvation.' She did this for many days. But when Paul perceived that the spirit operating in her was not the spirit of God, he became annoyed and turned and said to the spirit (note that Paul did not direct his anger at the girl, but at the spirit operating in her), 'I command you in the name of Jesus Christ to come out of her' (Acts 16:17 KJV). The Bible says that the spirit came out that same hour. But when her masters saw that their hope of profit was gone, they seized Paul and Silas and dragged them into the marketplace to the authorities and accused them of 'being Jews and troubling their city and teaching customs which were not lawful for them, being Romans, to receive or observe. Then the multitude rose up against them and tore their clothes and commanded them to be beaten with rods. And when they had laid many stripes on them, they threw them into prison and fastened their feet in the stocks.

Paul And Silas Delivered By An Angel Of God

But in the middle of the night, Paul and Silas were praying and singing hymns to God, and the prisoners were listening to them. Suddenly there was a great earthquake, so that the foundations of the prison were shaken, and immediately all the doors were opened and everyone's chains were loosed. So the keeper of the prison, awaking from sleep and seeing the prison doors open, supposing the prisoners had fled, drew his sword and was about to kill himself.

But Paul called with a loud voice, saying, 'Do yourself no harm, for we are all here.'

Then he called for a light, ran in, and fell down trembling before Paul and Silas. He did not stop there, but brought them out and said, 'Sirs, what must I do to be saved?'

And they told him, 'Believe in the Lord Jesus Christ, and you will be saved, you and your household.'Then they spoke the Word of the Lord to them and to all who were in his house. And he took them the same hour of the night and washed their stripes. And immediately he and all his house were baptised. (Acts 16:1-34 NKJV)

What happened later is another story that glorified the name of the Lord. You can read to the end.

A Great Lesson To Learn

Wow, what a story. Observe here that they did not go complaining or questioning God for their calamities or anything of the sort, but resorted to praising the Lord, hence their victory. This can only happen when the Holy Spirit is your helper, that is, after you must have given your life to Christ There is a great power in the prayer of the righteous. The story is so interesting that I had to take time to narrate it. It is similar to the story of Queen Esther. God is supreme. He is all -powerful and all-knowing. Hallelujah.

David

David is another servant of God whose life was full of prayer to his God. This could be found in the book of Psalms. Though psalms are said to contain, among others, topics like jubilation, war, peace, worship, judgment, messianic prophecy, praise, and lamentation, I believe that majority of it is prayer, and David was a major contributor. Though psalms were often sung, David prayed so many prayers in psalms. However, I am going to choose just a few for illustration. For instance, we could see some of his prayers to God, even when his son Absalom pursued him and wanted to kill him. Some of the prayers of David could be found in the book of Psalms as follows: 'I cried unto the Lord with my voice, to help me and He heard me out of His holy hill. I laid me down and slept, I awaked, for the Lord sustained me. I will not be afraid of ten thousands of people that have set themselves against me round about' (Psalm 3:4-6 KJV). When God is on your side, you will have no need to be afraid. But you must call upon Him to help you. All the prayers of David can be found in the book of Psalms.

It is impossible for anyone to live without God; such a person will grope in the dark and be opened to evil afflictions of the devil and his agents. But you must attach yourself to a church where salvation through Christ is preached, by being a committed member. A committed Christian is one who obeys the Word of God in the Bible. God says in His Word: Walk before me and be holy, for I am holy. You cannot live in sin and expect God to be answering your prayer. You must endeavour to live a holy life: forgive your enemies, so that He can also forgive you your sins. This does not mean that when you are forgiven, you should backslide and commit sins and come back to ask for forgiveness. This is what some churches teach, and this is an abomination before the Lord. The Lord Jesus told the woman caught in adultery after He had forgiven her: 'Go and sin no more' (John 8:11 KJV).

CHAPTER THIRTY-TWO

The Lord Needs Your Faith

WRITING TO THE twelve tribes of Israel which were scattered abroad, James began by saying, 'Greetings, My brethren count it all joy when you fall into diverse trials [temptations]. Knowing that the testing of your faith produces patience. But let patience have its perfect work, that you may be perfect and complete, lacking nothing.' On faith, he taught that 'Faith without work is dead.' A dead faith is worse than no faith at all, but faith must be visible or tangible. Faith understands temptations; it will deliver us from our lusts and prevent us from sliding into sin. Faith obeys the Word of God and is patient, because without patience we cannot exercise faith.

James taught extensively on faith and prayer. He told us in his book that the effectual fervent prayer of the righteous one avails much: 'Confess your trespasses to one another, and pray for one another, that you may be healed.' The effectual fervent prayer of a righteous man avails much.

Elijah was a man with a nature like ours, and he prayed earnestly that it would not rain, and it did not rain on the land for three years and six months (James 5:16-

18 NKJV). The angels are always waiting to carry out the commands of a righteous man; the only hindrance to prayer therefore is that of righteousness (salvation) and holy living. Please you may refresh your memory on this by revisiting the chapter on salvation, in case you are not sure of what I mean here.

Faith Means Patience

It takes faith to believe God. The Bible says that faith is a substance: 'Now faith is the substance of things hoped for, the evidence of things not seen' (Heb. 11:1 NKJV). It says again: For without faith, it is impossible to please God. You cannot therefore pray effectively without faith in the· Word of God; therefore, let doubt be far away from you in order to receive from God.

Prayer is an act of worship; it draws you closer to your Creator, God Almighty. It enhances your relationship with Him. It should be a two-way communication, not a monologue or soliloquy. In other words, it should not be an activity of a single performer, but two, you and the Lord Jesus. Knowledge of the importance of prayer will always inspire you to pray, because 'Everything depends on prayer.' These were the words of the Lord to me. When the Lord gave me the ministry of prayer, it was not easy establishing it, because people were not responding. Then I went back to God in prayer and said, 'Lord, people are not responding. I mean, they are not coming.' And the Lord said to me, 'It is because they do not know that everything depends on prayer.' Is it any wonder then that Jesus was always praying when He was here on earth? If God our heavenly Father and our creator says that everything depends on prayer, what then are you waiting for? It follows that there is no other way by which you can get your problems solved. You do not have to depend on your pastor or anyone else to pray for you, because once you are born again, or washed with the shed blood on the cross of Calvary, you automatically have access to God; therefore if you live a holy lifestyle, and a life of obedience to the Word of God, and belong to a church where salvation through Christ is preached, your prayers shall be answered.

With the assistance of the Holy Spirit, which Jesus shall send to help you once you give your life to Him, your prayer cannot be hindered by anyone, not even the devil. But you must know that it is not going to be automatic; patience must be exercised. All you will need to do is pray and believe or exercise your faith in God, and He will do it in His own time. God knows the right time to answer your prayer. Having said that, you will have to be a member of a living Church, where salvation through the Lord Jesus Christ is preached and taught. Again, you have to read your Bible daily, at least five chapters a day until you have read through the entire Bible. It is important to pray and invite the Holy Spirit to help you so that God can open your eyes to see wonderous things in His Word. Otherwise, you may read and not comprehend what you read, or the Bible may appear to you like a history book. Through your prayer, the living Word of God will work in your life. Your prayer life will also need to improve on a daily basis, at least three times a day: morning, afternoon, and in the evening before bedtime, in order to achieve a better result. Do not allow the devil to deceive you by telling you, Don't worry, God knows your problem. Therefore, you don't need to pray.' He is very cunning. This is a lie from the pit of hell; therefore, resist him and take your problems to God, because He is always waiting for you to bring your problems to Him.

Jesus asked the two blind men who went to Him for healing, 'What they would want Him to do for them,' even when He saw that they were blind, the reason being that He wanted to involve them in the process. In other words, Jesus wanted to test their faith. The blind men answered, 'We want to receive our sight.' Jesus asked them again, 'Do you believe that I can heal you?" And they answered, 'We believe!' (Matt. 9:28 KJV). Jesus will not do anything without your consent; this is why you must tell Him your problems yourself.

Prayer is very fundamental in the life of a believer. Apart from praying for your individual needs, you have more than a thousand and one things to pray for and to pray about in this turbulent world, for instance, your family, relations, friends, neighbours, communities, your nation, and even the world at large. God can use your prayer to bring peace in any part of the world, starting from your family. You should therefore not allow yourself to be manipulated by the enemy, the devil, through doubts and feelings of inferiority about what God can use your prayer to do.

At the beginning of this book, I told you how much regard the Lord accords this book in your hands. I did not know until, I heard a voice telling me thus: 'Please release my book.' Then I wondered, 'Which book?' It was at that point that I realised it was the Lord talking to me.

Then He pleaded with me saying, 'Please release my prayer book.' This shows how important the Lord regards this book. This is why you should regard this book as a prayer manual.

CHAPTER THIRTY-THREE

A Brief Look into the Book of Revelation

T HE BOOK OF Revelation was written by John. He was given a revelation when he was on exile on the island of Patmos. John was an apostle of Jesus Christ, the son of Zebedee (Matt. 10:2). He was a church leader and versed in the scripture; he was well known to the seven churches of Asia Minor, a deeply religious and holy man of God, who was fully convinced that the Christian faith would triumph over the demonic forces at work in the world. It is believed that John wrote the book of Revelation by himself, though he simply identified himself as John; please refer to Revelation 1:1, 1:4, 1:9, 22:8. The book of Revelation is basically on prophetic events, or what is today known as the last things, or eschatology. Its title means unveiling or disclosure, which in Greek is known as Apokalypsis Iesou Christou, meaning Revelation of Jesus Christ. The book of Revelation was given to John on the island of Patmos while he was in exile, to give to the seven churches in Asia, namely Ephesus, Smyrna, Pergamos, Thyatira, Sardis, Philadelphia, Laodicea.

The above could not have happened if John were not a praying disciple. People hate to pray until they are in trouble. My question is this: Can such prayers be answered? If you don't pray regularly, the chances are that you may not know how and when to pray. You are only living at the mercy of the devil, who can take your life anytime he wishes. God's grace is keeping everyone, but you should not take God's grace for granted, because the enemy can strike anytime. The Bible says that life is like a vapour. This means that we can lose it suddenly. Jesus says that, "The enemy comes not but to steal, kill, and to destroy". He steals you when he stops you from going to Church to worship God. He kills you (spiritually) when you backslide from going to church and when you stop obeying the Holy Spirit. He then destroys you when you die in this state, because this means you are going straight to hell. Don't mind those who say you will come back into this world in a different form, maybe tree, rat, and all sorts of things. These are all the lies of the devil, because the Bible says that, "Man is destined to die once and, after that, judgement," (Heb. 9:27 NIV). This is what the devil does not want you to believe, so that he can continuously accuse you before God, just as he accused Job.

The revealing stories in the book of Revelation (which, you will agree with me, is a very vital book in the Bible, because in it contains everything that will take place in the later years or days, though some must have been fulfilled and some are still being fulfilled) which were revealed to John in Patmos island. I believe that was because John was a praying disciple and also knowledgeable in the doctrines of Christ.

May I remind you that every believer is the temple of God; therefore, you are the Church of Christ. Nate also that angels are assigned to every church; as a believer, you should be conscious of your guiding angels and put them to work whenever necessary. However, for this to be effective, ensure that you are in the right standing with the Lord. In other words you should be obedient to the doctrines of Christ.

CHAPTER THIRTY-FOUR

Those Who God Uses

G OD DOES NOT prefer one to another, but as many as believe and call upon Him, He accepts. Once God accepts you, you will not imagine the extent to which He can use you. All that you will be expected to do is to live a life of obedience to the Word of God. The only way to get to know His will, is to read the King James version of the Bible, which is the original source of the Word of God. Some translated versions have omitted some vital parts of the original Bible; therefore, always refer to the original as you read.

If one is privileged to be called by God to serve, such a person should endeavour to serve to the satisfaction of the Lord, and not use the opportunity to serve oneself. On 22 June 2019, I watched a program on the Revelation Television, in London titled 'Billy Graham TV.' In the program Billy Graham testified how he doubted God's existence at a stage, even as an evangelist. I believe that this must have been the work of the enemy, the devil, who was attempting to make him to disbelieve God. According to Billy Graham, when the doubt arose in his mind, he decided to pray to God to assure him of His existence, and after the prayer, he found himself in tears, and his faith in God increased tremendously. This is the way God operates. God may have revealed Himself to him during that prayer. Those who say they do not believe in the existence of God should take note of this.

Billy Graham, as we know, was the greatest evangelist who ever lived. As I watched his funeral service, I heard the Lord saying audibly to me, 'Job well done'. I had no doubt that the Lord was referring to Pastor Billy Graham's evangelical performance. on earth. This is what every servant of God should aspire for: to be commended and accepted by the Lord at the end of his or her service on earth.

Warning: One should besure that God has called one to serve before delving into it; otherwise, the devil will take advantage of you and start using you. This is the reason why there are so many false prophets, because the devil knows the genuine servants of God, as well as those fake ones.

They Have Taken Him

This episode contrasts with that of Billy Graham. It concerns news of the death of a man of God, some years ago. I could not believe it, because he was a very active minister of the gospel. I was terribly shaken on hearing the news of his demise, because I was a partner in his ministry. This news did not quite sink, hence one day, I went to God in prayer concerning it. During my prayer, I enquired from the Lord Jesus to reveal the truth to me, and the Lord spoke the above words: 'They have taken him.' I further enquired from the Lord who the 'they' are. And the Lord answered, 'The enemy!' Still in doubt and became even more shaken. I asked again, 'Who?' And the Lord Jesus responded again, 'Satan.'

This man was a very vibrant man of God; and therefore, it wasn't easy for me to believe that Satan could take him, hence I continued to enquire from the Lord as to what had happened to him. The Lord said, 'Sin.' I retorted, 'Sin? What sin?' Again the Lord answered, "Sin of immorality.' This was unbelievable because I would have staked my life to deny that this man would indulge in such sin. One can only say that it is God who knows the hidden things of the heart. At this time, the Lord roared, 'Funfair.' By now, you probably know who the man of God was. The Lord has instructed me to write about it, and preach against it, to warn His servants. I have preached on this in one of my programmes. I also wrote about it on Facebook. I am planning to write a book on it, as the Lord enables me. In a nutshell, men of God are turning the house of God into business and event centre. They forget that the accuser of the brethren, the devil, is always looking for opportunity to pull down the servants of God.

SUMMARY

THERE IS NOTHING that gives one comfort and peace of mind as knowing that you have access to God at any time. God indeed is love, in sending His Son to come and redeem mankind from the grip of the enemy, who is always looking for an opportunity to accuse man before God. He endeavours very hard to lure man into sin, after which he will accuse man before God. Hence the Lord admonishes His children to always resist him.

Now that you have known how important prayer is in your life, I do hope that you will take it serious in your Christian race, for it is only by doing this can you begin to enjoy heaven in this world; because all your problems will easily be solved by this knowledge. But be aware that knowledge alone cannot give you victory, but only by putting it into action. Remember that Jesus told His disciples, that some problems can only be solved by fasting and prayer. Forgiveness and living in love with our neighbours are powerful weapons which God uses in dealing with our problems. Please note that all mankind represent your neighbour.

As you have already known, prayer answers all your problems, and God can use your prayer to bring peace in this world. Apart from praying for your individual needs, you have more than a thousand and one things to pray for, in this turbulent world. For instance, your family, loved ones or relations, neighbours, communities, and even your nation and the world at large can be healed through your prayer.

At the beginning of this book, I told of how much the Lord holds this book in high esteem. I never knew, until one day I heard a voice telling me, 'Please release my book.' Then I wondered, and asked 'Which book?' It was then I realised that it was the Lord talking to me. Then He answered by saying, 'I can't wait for you to release my prayer book.' Jesus said: "Men ought always to pray, and not to faint." If God our heavenly Father, our creator, says everything depends on prayer, then what are you waiting for? You don't have to depend on your pastor or any other person to pray for you. As soon as you have given your life to Christ (washed with the blood of Jesus), you are automatically qualified to approach God in prayer, and your prayer cannot be hindered by anyone, not even the devil.

Having said that, you have to be a member of a local and living church where salvation through the Lord Jesus is taught. Second, you have to be a daily Bible reader of at least five chapters a day until you have covered the Bible. Each time before you start, invite the Holy Spirit to come and help you so that your eyes can be opened to behold wondrous things in it; otherwise, it will be like a history book to you. This way, the living Word of God will be made manifest and powerful in your life. God is always waiting for you to bring your problems to Him. I had earlier told you what the Lord Jesus told the two blind men who went to Him for healing: 'What do you want me to do for you?' He asked. Jesus saw that they were blind, but He still asked them that question. They answered, 'We want to receive our sight.' Jesus asked again, 'Do you believe that I can heal you?' Jesus wanted to test their faith as well as involve them in the process. Therefore always exercise your faith by taking your problems to the Lord. He is ever waiting and wanting to help you. Do not meditate on your problems rather meditate on His ability and willingness to help you.

CONCLUSION

I N CONCLUSION, I wish to affirm that God is ever faithful and always true to His promises. He is a prayer answering God. When you pray and it seems as if the answer will not come, be patient, and keep your faith up, and the answer will surely come. God is never late.

He says call on me in time of trouble and I will show you great and mighty thing which thou knowest not...(Jer. 33:3 KJV). When He eventually answers your prayer, never forget to testify openly in His great or small congregation; for this is how you can overcome the enemy.

In the book of Revelation it is said: And they overcame him by the blood of the lamb, and by the word of their testimony, (Rev.12:11, KJV). Spiritual sensitivity which the Holy Spirit imparts in us at the point of our conversion is the key to success in our Christian race.

It is a great privilege to be able to access God through prayer. I therefore encourage you to pray without ceasing.

Refrain engaging in careless and senseless conversations.

www.ingramcontent.com/pod-product-compliance
Lightning Source LLC
Chambersburg PA
CBHW071722120626
46550CB00001B/348